INSIDER'S
GUIDE
TO
MATERNITY
LEAVE

Real Stories And Expert Advice On Preparing For Work, Career, And Life After Baby

VICTORIA HEFTY

BABY BUMP MEDIA • PHILADELPHIA

For permission requests, write to the publisher at:
Baby Bump Media
2037 Chestnut Street
P.O. Box 2205
Philadelphia, PA 19103

The Insider's Guide to Maternity Leave/ Baby Bump Media/ Victoria Hefty—1st ed. ISBN-978-1544296616
Printed in the United States of America
First printing March 2017

To Karl, my number one fan.

Thank you to all of the women who trusted me to share your stories. I am deeply grateful.

FREE!

Sign up and receive a free digital file that includes the resources, checklists, and links featured in this book.

www.TheInsidersGuidetoMaternityLeave.com

CONTENTS

A Note From The Author

I wrote *The Insider's Guide To Maternity Leave* to help expectant mothers anticipate the challenges that may surround maternity leave and to offer fresh perspectives on what those challenges may mean for their jobs, career, and post-baby life.

Along with stories and tips from working moms on what they would do differently looking back, this book includes advice from experts and resources for additional research. The book also aims to help expectant mothers optimize the time before their due date to explore new professional interests.

The Insider's Guide To Maternity Leave deals with maternity leave in an honest, direct, the-stuff-no-one-talks-about way. It does not present an ideal view of what maternity leave should be but instead opens up about what maternity leave is *really* like for many women.

This book does not focus heavily on traditional postpartum topics such as newborn care, breastfeeding, etc. nor does it offer a comprehensive view of all things maternity leave. Instead, *The Insider's Guide To Maternity Leave* focuses on the issues that were most common or significant among the 300+ women that I interviewed and surveyed.

My hope is that in the midst of picking out baby names or decorating the nursery, you will read this book to anticipate better the potential challenges and find new inspiration for the possibilities.

- *Victoria Hefty*

vi

Preface

The idea for *The Insider's Guide to Maternity Leave* came from two conversations I had over the course of a day. First, I was texting a friend who works for a company in San Francisco and who is currently expecting her first child. I asked my friend if she was thinking about looking for a new job or changing careers once the baby came, and she responded with the following text:

> Looking into a new career crossed my mind briefly since I know this time period is a good time to think about that and do it. However, I really like my company (███████ has a great parental leave program and resources) and my boss is super supportive (she had her first last year and is due again in ████████) so I had no worries about that. I think my biggest concern will be transitioning back to work

I replied with a short version of my maternity leave story (Part II of this book) and told her that while it was wonderful that she had a supportive manager, that manager may not always be there. Therefore, it was critical to plan out and document everything related to her transition back to work, in case things changed while she was out on leave.

I wasn't trying to scare her by any means; I was just sharing what I had learned from my experience. She was grateful for the information and asked me to pass along any other tips that may be helpful.

Later that evening, I was talking to my husband about the conversation I had with the friend, and I said, "You know, I really wish someone would have told me that coming back from maternity leave was going to be so complicated and difficult. Looking back, I wish I had known more."

And that's when I knew I had to write this book. I didn't know how I was going to do it because I am a blogger—not a trained, professional writer. I didn't want to embarrass myself, but my intuition said I was on to something. Besides, I was my own customer, as I would have definitely bought this type of book had it been available when I was pregnant.

But I wanted to be sure, so I asked a few other first-time expectant mothers I knew, and they loved the concept. I created a couple of test surveys to confirm that I was indeed on the right track, and here we are, 300+ surveys and interviews later.

As someone who likes to be prepared, I had thought I had done what was needed to make the most of my maternity leave. Even so, unpredictable events, both in my work environment and within me as a new mother, changed my situation in a way that I did not see coming.

The stories, advice, and insights in this book will help you to prepare for the kinds of things that all-too-often can happen but are difficult (if not impossible) to foresee.

Even if you have the "perfect" maternity leave, the range of experiences will hopefully leave you inspired and more informed about the different possibilities that your maternity leave and the early days of motherhood can offer.

Please note that I didn't receive any form of compensation for featuring the experts, services, products, etc. mentioned in this book. These are all resources that I have either personally used, found through my research, or were referred to me through reputable sources.

Part I: I Wish I Had Known To...

CHAPTER

1. Research My Maternity Leave Policy

"Be very clear on the specifics of your company maternity policy and ask questions. Be informed on policies in place both legally and on a company level, so that you know your rights. Speak to HR and document EVERYTHING."

~ Anna, age 34, California

Why is it important for an expectant mom to under‟ stand her company's maternity leave policy? There is a lot of misinformation about maternity leave because policies vary by state, by company, and even by man‐ ager. This often leads to first-time moms getting caught up in the excitement of the baby and assuming that a salaried, professional job will cover a good por‐ tion of their leave in some way, and the situation will work itself out.

However, as with compensation packages, most companies rarely have one standard maternity leave package. Your maternity leave experience is subject to how long you have been at the company, your bene‐ fits, your role at the company, your manager's atti‟ tude and expectations, etc. And as with your compen‐ sation package, discussing your maternity leave poli‐ cy openly with coworkers can be taboo or in some cases not allowed, depending on your company.

The whole experience can leave expectant moms feeling very vulnerable, and the lack of transparency in the process and policies tends to breed anxiety and uncertainty.

Family and Medical Leave Act (FMLA)

Although there have been a few companies recently in the news (for example, American Express, Patago‟ nia, Chobani, and Ikea) that are offering twenty-plus weeks of paid maternity leave, the majority of com‐ panies are not even close to this, both in the number of weeks they allow an employee to take away from work and in offering paid leave.

In actuality, only 12% of U.S. workers in the private sector can get paid family leave through their employer, this according to a 2012 study by the Department of Labor. For more information, visit the Department of Labor's website at www.dol.gov.

The reality is that for most women, "maternity leave" is just another way of saying your time off from work will be covered using a mixture of paid leave, which can be a combination of short-term disability (STD), vacation or paid time off (PTO) days, and sick days. The Family and Medical Leave Act (FMLA) relates to the unpaid portion of maternity leave.

"I don't think you should use the term "maternity leave". I never do. Saying those words means people can forget the fact there is no such thing. I had short-term disability, used all my vacation, and had to forfeit salary and bonus."

~ Jennifer, age 39, Maryland

"I pocketed all of my sick and vacation days for an entire year, plus two weeks of paid leave, and I still needed to take a week of unpaid leave. It was a major stress."

~ Denise, age 31, Florida

"I had to use up all my vacation time while on leave so when I came back to work I didn't have any time left for sick days"

~ *Susan, age 28, California*

"I worked up until my due date, so if you aren't doing manual labor, I would suggest doing that. It gives you more time on the back end to spend with the baby, as opposed to starting maternity leave 1-2 weeks before."

~ *Mia, age 32, New York*

In order to understand your company's maternity leave policy, you must understand FMLA as it is one of the most misquoted and misunderstood components of maternity leave.

According to the U.S. Department of Labor: "The Family and Medical Leave Act ("FMLA") provides certain employees with up to 12 workweeks of unpaid, job-protected leave a year, and requires group health benefits to be maintained during the leave as if employees continued to work instead of taking leave."

What most people don't know is that to be eligible for FMLA leave, an employee must work for a covered employer *and* have worked for that employer for at least 12 months; *and* have worked at least 1,250 hours during the 12 months prior to the start of the

FMLA leave; *and* work at a location where at least 50 employees are employed at the location or within 75 miles of the location. A covered employer is a public agency, including local, state, and federal employers, or a private sector employer who employs 50 or more employees.

It's not surprising, then, that according to the Department of Labor, "More than 40% of U.S. workers don't meet all of FMLA's requirements, and even if they do, many can't afford to take unpaid leave."

> "I remember reading through the company policy quickly and assuming I was covered. I didn't know until much later that I would be required to continue paying my health insurance premiums while I was out even though I was on unpaid leave. It was tough financially."
>
> ~ *Kathy, age 36, Pennsylvania*

> "I didn't even qualify for FMLA because my company wasn't big enough, even though I was in a salaried position. I couldn't believe it."
>
> ~ *Stephanie, age 35, Pennsylvania*

> "I was advised if I took anything outside of the 12 weeks FMLA, I would be terminated immediately."
>
> ~ *Novella, age 29, Texas*

"I wish I would have known that they could fire you while you are on leave! I expected them to hold my job, but the week before I was ready to come back to work, they replaced me with a new hire."

~ Arlene, age 39, Oregon

Mom Spotlight: Rachel, Director of Global Marketing

Rachel, Director of Global Marketing in the Pharmaceutical Industry

On my last day of work before maternity leave, I felt equally overjoyed and sad. I'm forty-two, and I've worked in one way, shape, or form since I was twelve years old. It was bittersweet to have accomplished so much work-wise but also to finally have a dream come true to be a mom.

Unexpected News:

I did not expect my job to be eliminated while I was on maternity leave. I was on unpaid leave because I wasn't at my job long enough to be eligible for FMLA. I joined the company while pregnant and was on a new-product launch team for a drug that never made it to FDA filing because of negative data. So they shut down the whole thing.

I had no job to go back to and was not in the position to network and interview to find another one because I was on maternity leave. I regret that I wasn't able to network or figure out how to navigate finding a new position within the company.

Short-Term Disability (STD)

For most women, "paid maternity leave" is pri⁻marily covered through Short-Term Disability (STD) benefit payments and then supplemented with vacation and sick days. While no expectant mother wants to view their pregnancy (and baby!) as a disability, this less than ideal term is a good reminder to scrutinize your STD policy the same way you would your medical insurance benefits.

STD is separate from your company's medical in⁻surance and often outsourced to a STD company such as MetLife. For example, when I called the benefits department at my company to find out more about my maternity leave policy, I was given a number to call a third-party vendor.

This separation often leads to a lot of back and forth between what Human Resources or the benefits department at a company says to expectant moms, versus what the STD representative says or needs. If your company doesn't have a streamlined process, it might be easy for you to miss critical information and deadlines.

Don't assume that your contact in Human Re⁻sources will tell you everything you need to know, so be proactive. Research federal, state, and local STD laws, especially if you work for a company that has offices in two or more states.

"I work for a small business that had no maternity leave policy in place. Even worse, although my job contract listed short term disability insurance as a benefit, it became clear after I was pregnant that the company never purchased coverage for me even though it was listed as a benefit.

The negotiations that followed were extremely un⁻ comfortable, and I only received the minimum (2 weeks) even though I know I would have been entitled to more if I'd had the STD benefit. They made me feel like I was asking for special treat⁻ ment, instead of what I was entitled to. In the future, it would be preferable to know that the pieces were in place before I was expecting."

~ *Carolyn, age 28, New Jersey*

Lastly, if you are reading this book you are proba⁻ bly already pregnant but the following information may be helpful for your friends or family members that are thinking of starting a family.

Many young, first-time expectant moms assume they have STD as part of their job, especially if they barely review their benefit packages (which happens quite a lot). The problem is, if you don't have STD and you suddenly find out you are pregnant, it will most likely be too late to purchase a policy. That is, you must have a STD policy *before* you get pregnant.

"My short term disability was denied because my employer said I was pregnant before coverage started. I didn't even know they could do that."

~ *Faye, age 33, Louisiana*

Resource Spotlight: Leave Logic

The following advice is from LeaveLogic, a company that provides apps and solutions to help employees and compa‾ nies plan, execute, and manage maternity/family leave processes.

The advice and tips below are intended to simplify the maternity leave planning process by helping you to patch together the applicable laws, benefits, and policies available. While a good starting point, you should discuss specific policy and benefit eligibility with your human resources department.

Understand your rights.

Determine if you are eligible for FMLA. Use the checklist below, but always confirm eligibility with your HR department:
- Your employer has over 50 employees living within 75 miles
- OR your employer is a public agency (federal, state, or local)
- You have been employed for at least 12 months by your employer
- You have worked at least 1,250 hours in the last 12 months

Determine if your state, city, or county has a separate fami‾ ly leave law or STD policy. Currently, only a handful of state and local policies have been implemented, but more are expected in the absence of a federal paid family leave policy. Each policy varies, but many will provide a percent of income replacement through short-term disability (STD) insurance.

Know you have rights. Both parents should have access to job-protected leave, even if it is unpaid. The Equal Employment Opportunity Commission (EEOC) has guidance on pregnancy-related issues.

Understand your benefits.

Company Benefits/Policy Questions:
   • Does your company offer paid maternity leave and/or STD? If yes, for how long and at what percentage of pay?
   • If your state offers paid leave, does the state benefit have to be used first?
   • Is there a waiting period before you can collect benefits/payments? If yes, can you use vacation/sick/personal days to fill the gap?
   • Are there limitations to how many vacation/sick/personal days you are able to use?
   • Does your company have a return-to-work assistance/flexibility program option?

Insurance Questions:
   • What are your health insurance carrier's benefits, including out-of-pocket maximum and deductibles for pre-natal care, labor, and delivery costs? Note:

This information could be dependent on your due date, so confirm with your insurance company.

• What pre-natal and newborn screening tests are covered by your insurance?

• What local hospitals are in your insurance poli‾ cy's network?

• What is the breast pump reimbursement process?

EAPS, FSAs, and HSAs (The Benefits Alphabet Soup)

• Look into what Employee Assistance Programs (EAP) are available. These could include anything from legal coverage and postpartum depression, to childcare matching services and free breast milk shipping.

• If you haven't looked into your FSA and HSA options yet, now is a good time!

Don't forget your return to work plan!

This is incredibly important. Find out what flexible arrangements are available or might be possible. You *can* negotiate. Look at what you and your growing family need to effectively ease back into your career.

Remember, just because a flexible work plan hasn't been done, doesn't mean it can't be done, so ask!

We also offer an app for parental leave planning. For more information, visit www.leavelogic.com

Mom Spotlight: Nicole, Physical Therapist

Nicole, Physical Therapist in the Healthcare Industry

I was already 3 months pregnant when I realized my job did not offer paid leave. Mostly my own fault for doing no research. I had just assumed my maternity leave was paid in some capacity, as several of my co-workers had taken 13 weeks of leave and never mentioned anything.

It took me watching a Mother's Day segment on Jon Oliver to realize all I was getting was FMLA. So after the initial shock and intense conversation with my husband—we were lucky enough to be able to move some finances around to allow us to survive me taking 13 weeks off for work.

My expectations vs. reality:

I imagined nothing but three months of baby bliss, happiness, and some free time during naps to get things done at home. I envisioned myself completing projects around the house, cooking healthy meals every night, taking leisurely strolls around Philly with my daughter every morning…

Turns out I highly underestimated the physical toll of having a baby, and my first two to three weeks were spent strictly recovering. One "stroll" to the first pediatrician visit had me unable to move for two days. I think for the first eight weeks, I operated on half-asleep autopilot and barely remember any of it. I wish I'd gone into it prepared to hunker down, rest, and bond.

Unexpected lessons:

I was surprised at how much time was needed just to heal, recover, and come to terms with the gigantic changes my body and my life had just gone through—both physically and psychologically.

I learned that even though you've got a brand new child, maternity leave is lonely as you navigate your new role, identity, and the loss of who you were. I regret not reaching out to local new mom/breastfeeding support groups. I think having more contact with women in the same position would have been both beneficial and enjoyable.

Returning to work:

Maternity leave changed my mind both about being a stay-at-home mom (which I always thought I wanted) and about being a working mom (which I always thought I'd easily give up).

Due to finances, I had to return to work full time following my leave—and I was shocked at how good it felt to be back. I didn't realize how much I enjoyed the "professional me" and missed that role while I was home.

Expert Advice: Navigating Maternity Leave Policy

The following advice is from Amy Johnson, a former HR Manager for a Consumer Goods and Retail Industry company with 30,000+ part time, seasonal, and full time employees worldwide.

My very first suggestion to navigating maternity leave at work is to research your company's policy, including short-term and long-term disability. You may not get paid for a lot of weeks, but you may be eligible for more than you think. Yet a lot of people don't research the details to take advantage of that.

When I was in HR, we had a few women who were pregnant and did not file paperwork for short-term disability—even though they qualified—to cover some of their expenses while they were out on maternity leave. Don't make assumptions about what you think you have or don't have. My advice is to research heavily, go back through your benefits package, and ask questions!

Talk to your doctor, and make sure his or her office staff is on top of their paperwork. We would get a lot of calls from new moms who were very upset because their short-term disability or FMLA or something had not been approved because we were waiting on doctor paperwork. Doctors can take weeks to fill out and sign papers if you don't follow-up, so again, don't assume it's been taken care of. Call and make sure the physician's office has done their part.

Announcing your pregnancy.

I would recommend announcing your pregnancy to HR first so that you can have an open discussion about the company's maternity leave policies. That being said, once you start putting a maternity leave plan in place, it is best to speak directly to your man⁻ ager about it. HR handles all of the paperwork and all the legalities, but the manager is the person you work with on a daily basis.

Some people will provide only HR with the dates they plan to take and return from maternity leave, as⁻ suming HR is responsible for passing on that informa- tion to their manager. The truth is, we get over- whelmed and are pulled in many directions. Critical information falls through the cracks, so it's important that you communicate things such as maternity leave dates, transition plans, etc. with your manager.

Transition back to work.

Be straightforward and upfront with any limita⁻ tions that you may have. One situation we used to run into all the time was new moms coming back to work and not telling us that they still hadn't healed after their C-section (caesarian). They would come back and be limited in the amount of work they could take on, and they were afraid to say anything.

Also, make a phone call two weeks before you re⁻ turn from maternity leave to make sure everything is in order. Something at your company could have changed while you were gone—something you might not be expecting—so it's better to check in with your manager before your first day back from leave.

I interviewed a New York City-based employment attor-ney, and here are some tips that she provided about nav-igating maternity leave at work.

Talk with your healthcare provider.

I was fortunate enough to go through my pregnan-cy feeling full of energy, clear headed, and cheerful up until my last few days before giving birth. But each pregnancy is different. Sometimes, women suffer ex-treme morning sickness (hyperemesis gravidarum), preeclamsia, high blood pressure, back pain, or other issues that may limit their ability to perform their job at 100%.

Right from your first appointment, you should be starting a dialogue with your provider about your job duties, any anticipated hardships, and come up with a plan that you are comfortable with. Although you cannot plan for everything, an early dialogue with your provider can be helpful in giving you the infor-mation and confidence you need to continue in the workplace.

What and when to tell your employer.

When I was pregnant, I waited as long as possible to tell my employer, until I was at least 5 months pregnant. There were a few reasons for this. One, I was on a big case that required me to work long hours. I was afraid that if I told my employer I was pregnant, they would feel funny about my working long hours and then potentially limit my involvement on the case. Although these adjustments can be coming from a good place, they can be problematic and sometimes illegal.

There may be good reasons for telling your employer sooner than I did—for example, maintaining goodwill so that the company has as long as possible to plan for your absence or if you need any accommodations to make sure that you are taken care of. Telling your employer puts them on notice that you are pregnant and may entitle you to certain protections under the law.

Know your rights.

If your employer has more than 15 employees, you are protected under the federal Pregnancy Discrimination Act. The PDA requires that covered employers treat women affected by pregnancy, childbirth, or related medical conditions in the same manner as other applicants or employees who are similar in their ability or inability to work. Under the PDA, pregnant workers are protected from discrimination based on current pregnancy, past pregnancy, and potential pregnancy. If your employer has less than 15 employees, then you still may be protected under state or local laws. The Equal Employment Opportunity Commission ("EEOC") website is a good place to start for a basic understanding of your rights under federal law. See also "State Family and Medical Leave Laws" at www.ncsl.org.

Know when to call in backup.

If something doesn't "feel right" (i.e. your manager or employer took you off that big case, you are sud-denly getting bad reviews, you told your employer that you're pregnant, and you are fired the next week), talk to a lawyer. Be clear about your goals. If you want to continue working for the company, serv-ing them with a lawyer's letter—or a lawsuit—may not be the best way to get there. I've had a lot of suc-cess negotiating "behind the scenes" for clients, help-ing clients to frame their requests in certain ways, helping clients to talk through potential accommoda-tions (modified schedule, a chair with better back support, etc.) that will make their lives a little easier.

One thing that is often difficult is what happens when your employer unilaterally makes modifica-tions for you because "you're pregnant—you should relax!" This is not okay and is potentially illegal, as the employer is modifying your employment because of your pregnancy. In that situation, a simple and di-rect response can go a long way. *"Hi, ___, thank you so much for your concern. I am very lucky to have a coworker/ boss like you who is looking out for my well being during my pregnancy. The reality is that I am feeling great and am excited to keep working on ___ projects. If at any time I need any kind of accommodation, I will certainly let you know, and we can discuss it at that point. Thanks again for everything, ___."*

Additional Advice + Strategies

Talk to co-workers.

Find a trusted co-worker who has taken maternity leave at your company and offer to take her out to coffee/lunch for a chat. It helps if she is or was at or close to your position level when she went on leave, but it's not a requirement. While every woman will have a different experience that is at least in part dependent upon her role and her manager, you can still learn some great information this way.

Be respectful of the information your co-worker provides. This means, unless you have explicit per⁻mission, try not to reference your co-worker's specific experience when talking to HR or your manager about possible work arrangements for you. Use your research and knowledge gained from your chat instead to help inform the types of questions you ask.

Questions to consider asking your co-worker.
• Was there anything that surprised her about your company's maternity leave policy?
• What did she do work-related in preparing to go on maternity leave that was particularly helpful?
• Was she allowed to work from home at all prior to having the baby? What about when transitioning back from leave?
• Does she have tips on how you can best transi⁻tion back to work?

Save up your vacation and sick days.

Unless you are one of the fortunate women who will receive paid leave for 12-plus weeks, strongly consider saving up all your vacation/sick days, as other moms have suggested. This may mean forgoing out-of-town weddings or adjusting your vacation/baby-moon plans, but you will be thankful to have extra days available in case you need them.

Confirm with your benefits department about how many vacation or sick days you can roll over from the year prior, so you can optimize the number of days you have available.

Keep your paperwork organized.

Keep a record of all the types of paperwork you need to fill out. Include deadlines, outstanding questions you may have, and who/what needs to be approved in order for forms to be considered complete. If possible, print or scan/upload/email copies of any paperwork you fill out.

"Don't wait until the third trimester to look into your maternity leave policy. Complications such as being put on bed rest or going into labor prematurely can happen, and you don't want to be in that position. Prepare early, and prepare for the unexpected!"

~ *Jessica, age 33, Massachusetts*

"Ensure your employer has met all the deadlines and completed all paperwork in timely manner for your STD claims or else you won't get paid! You have to check on everything, and do not assume others are on top of things."

~ *Donna, age 31, Tennessee*

"Turn in maternity leave paperwork ON TIME. I can't state that enough. These disability companies are not playing when it comes to claims and will find any reason to deny or delay payment."

~ *Jacquelyn, age 40, New York*

"Most people don't think about it, but along with STD, I recommend all women strongly consider getting long term disability insurance before getting pregnant. You just never know what will happen, and the price is nominal relative to the peace of mind financially if something does happen."

~ *Claudia, age 30, Illinois*

CHAPTER

2. Create a Maternity Plan Early in the Process

"Let your employer know far ahead of time when you expect to be out, and negotiate with them early in. You have more leverage earlier in the process than say when you are rushing to get things done before your leave starts"

~ *Gloria, age 37, Colorado*

Don't wait until your last month of pregnancy to start creating a maternity leave/transition plan for your co-workers or team. Give yourself plenty of time to train and pass along your responsibilities. Based on my interviews, having the option to create a flexible work arrangement can be critical for new mothers when it comes time to successfully transition back to work.

The key is to explore potential arrangements that work for you and your role well *before* you go on maternity leave. If your manager doesn't support working from home once a week, ask your manager or Human Resources if you can do any of the following the first 3 to 6 months after you return from maternity leave:

- *Work from home once every two weeks.*
- *Come in early and leave the office early one day a week – for example, come in at 7:00 a.m. and leave at 3:00 p.m.*
- *Work condensed hours, Monday through Thursday, and then leave early on Friday*

If the answer is no, at least you tried, and then you can make an informed decision about what that means for you and your job.

"Ease back into work, starting 2 weeks before going back full time. Save up some PTO and transition back gradually."

~ *Olive, age 38, Delaware*

"My company was great with my maternity leave. They allowed me to work from home after my leave was up, so I was able to stay home for six months after my little one was born. Talk to your employer about your situation, and see if they can facilitate working from home after your leave."

~ Janice, age 34, Georgia

Expert Advice: Why You Need a Maternity Leave Plan

The following advice is from Romy Newman, Co-Founder of Fairygodboss, a website designed to help professional women get the inside scoop on maternity leave policies, pay, corporate culture, benefits, and work flexibility.

It may not be obvious why you need a plan, but if you consider the fact that you may be gone for a sub¯ stantial amount of time from your employer, it makes sense to think about how to prepare your team, colleagues, and employer for your departure and return from maternity leave.

For those of you lucky enough to work at an em¯ ployer where extended leave is part of the policy, you may be away from work for several months. A plan can help you in the following ways:

Help you organize yourself.

First and foremost, your maternity leave plan is for yourself. You should look at your due date and when that falls relative to your work projects and deadlines. Whatever you can anticipate now will save you stress and unnecessary anxiety, particularly if you have an earlier-than-expected birth.

When do you expect to start your leave? Who will cover for you, and how? How much do you plan on staying in touch with your team? These are the details to outline, and they are important for you to think through, whether or not anyone asks you to share your plan.

Impress your managers and colleagues.

One of the reasons a maternity leave plan can be so impressive is that not everyone will create one. By listing the information everyone could possibly want to know surrounding your departure and return, you've saved yourself a lot of awkward questions and provided a single point of reference for anyone interested in how you plan on staying in touch—if at all—and who will be covering for the various aspects of your job.

Provide a list of tactical and practical information to those stepping in to cover for you.

Put yourself in your boss' and co-workers' shoes. If one of them were to leave the company for 8-12 weeks, what would you want to know? If someone needs to contact you for emergencies, how should they reach you? Will you plan on regular phone conversations if you're a manager? Do you plan on delegating all your work in advance to others, and if there is more than one person covering for you, who is responsible for what issues? Consider this document a navigational tool for others in your absence.

Set your colleagues' and boss' expectations.

Many times, managers and colleagues feel awk‐ward asking how much you plan on accomplishing before your leave, and even how long you plan on being away. This is because nobody wants to make open assumptions about how long your leave will be or put pressure on you to do more than you can.

One of the benefits of creating a plan is to set these expectations long before they become an issue.

Before your departure.

We suggest starting with your due date—and shar‐ing it—in the document. To create the initial part of your maternity leave plan, plan on working backward for roughly two months prior.

Set a schedule of what projects and tasks you plan on accomplishing before you leave. Don't be shy about bragging about the achievements you plan on making during the period before you leave. This doc‐ument is, in many ways, proof that you're not leaving anyone in the lurch.

The time during your leave.

Create a list of all your ongoing responsibilities that cannot be completed prior to your leave. If you have direct reports, assign them some portion of your tasks. Notify them, and set up a time to talk about their additional duties, and then detail your mutual understanding in your maternity leave plan. Get your manager's approval, if necessary, and then explain that this is a way for you to assess your direct reports' ability to grow into new areas. This should be something they consider a career opportunity.

If there isn't anyone who can cover for you, you may need to be explicit about that, and ask for help from your manager or HR department with respect to hiring a temporary replacement. Your employer will appreciate that you were proactive in anticipating their needs rather than simply walking out and announcing that nobody is around who can do your job. If you give them time, they may be able to hire someone on a temporary or contract basis. You can even volunteer to help select that person by interviewing them and training them.

State how long you plan to take for maternity leave. We understand that feelings and situations may change. Premature births happen, as do situations where moms feel as if they need to return to work early due to exceptional circumstances at work. But if you don't state your expected duration, you're creating unnecessary uncertainty. Plans are not written in stone, and they are there to help everyone understand your intentions.

Part of what you should anticipate is whether you will have to—or want to—do any work while you're out on leave. If you're a manager, you may want weekly email or phone check-ins with your team. Or maybe you want to keep in touch with your boss, but only after the first month you're away or the two weeks before your return, so you can catch up.

Be clear with everyone what you want in terms of contact and when you want to be contacted. Whatever you say is fine, but the clarity will be much appreciated.

Your return from leave.

If you plan on phasing back your return to work as opposed to coming back on a full schedule, you should negotiate that, and present this part of the plan separately with your manager. You may want to start by coming back "early" but working part-time or remotely initially, just to get back into the swing of things.

If you plan on asking for a different schedule after you have a baby, don't try to sneak it into this document and simply hand this paper over to your boss. Have a conversation with your manager about that, and make that the focal point of your discussion about your maternity leave plan.

Addressing how you will do your work under a new schedule and presenting it in terms of a business case and your employer's point of view are important. Negotiating for more job flexibility when you return from maternity leave is something to do quite carefully in order to maximize your chances of success.

If you plan on working full-time but limiting or changing your travel plans upon your return, this is something to bring up before you take maternity leave. Also, you may want to think about whether you want to breastfeed, as this can require time during your day and impact your travel. It's completely possible to travel and pump, but it requires some

planning, and some employers even offer reimbursement or services that facilitate the shipping of breast
milk.

In sum, a maternity leave document is something
you should present to your manager in order to help
yourself, your boss, and your colleagues.

Once approved, your plan—or a condensed ver⁻
sion of it—should be shared with relevant colleagues
and co-workers, so they know what you're planning
on doing before, during, and after your return. While
this isn't a plan that's written in stone, it will help you
get organized and impress your coworkers.

This document may not make sense for everyone,
but depending on your length of leave and type of
job, it can help smooth the transition away from the
office and provide tactical and logistical details that
will make you and everyone else feel much better
about your time away.

Peace of mind during maternity leave is priceless,
so it's worth front-loading some thought and plan⁻
ning before your baby arrives!

You can also read the article, *The Office Maternity
Leave Checklist for the "Type A" Professional*, on
Fairygodboss.com, which covers pretty much every
last detail we think matters for the transition from the
office to being at home with your baby.

Mom Spotlight: Jennifer, Manager of Endowments

Jennifer, Manager of Endowments

for a Museum

My job doesn't pay any maternity benefits or health benefits during maternity leave, so the fif‐ teen weeks leave I took were all unpaid. That left such a sour taste in my mouth, that I have decided to continue to fight my company on it, even though it's not directly relevant to me anymore.

When I first became pregnant, I asked to work part-time upon my return to work. I asked to work four days per week, and then I offered to work full-time over four days, and then I offered to do that arrangement only until baby turned one year old.

All options were rejected.

I don't feel loyalty to my employer now that I am back to work, and I am job searching. I love my job, but I don't love that my employer is not sup‐ portive of working mothers.

Last day of work before maternity leave:

I was in labor on my last day of work before maternity leave. At a morning non-stress test appointment, the nurse told me, "Honey, this is nothing to write home about," after looking at my contractions on the monitor.

But I just knew. I rushed home and packed my hospital bag (that I should have packed weeks earlier). I then worked a full day—the hardest and fastest I have ever worked in my life—finishing up assignments and making a guide for my teammates at work to keep up with my assignments during my maternity leave.

Sure enough, baby was born the next morning at 8:30 a.m., almost exactly twenty-four hours after the contractions had started. They were, in fact, definitely something to write home about!

Breastfeeding:

The only thing I wish I had done differently is to have given up on breastfeeding earlier. The "breast is best" movement sucked me in and led to five stressful, exhausting, sad weeks of attempting breastfeeding—plus two failed tongue tie corrections, syringe feeding to avoid alleged "nipple confusion", and pumping around the clock. I won't do that again.

Mom Spotlight: Casey, Advancement Staff

Casey, Advancement Staff in the Education Industry

Leading up to my second leave, I worked with my supervisor to find a temp who could fill in for me while I was gone. Knowing there was someone at the office to keep certain projects moving was a relief, and I thought about work very little.

My maternity leave:

I thought I would be a stay-at-home-mom in train‐ing, so to speak, while I was home with my kids. I anticipated keeping on top of chores and cooking while starting some DIY home projects.

I thought I would take a lot of day trips with the baby and enjoy quality time with my newborn and husband while he was home for a short period of time. I thought I'd get out of the house and join lo‐cal new mom groups and make new friends.

What actually happened: I was too horrified about the idea of having to nurse in public or change a diaper blowout in a public restroom to even leave the house!

And even though newborns do a lot of eating and sleeping in the first month or two, I was too ex⁻ hausted to keep up with all of the chores!

Another chance:

I am lucky enough to have a second maternity leave under my belt, so I had a chance to do it again. The second time around, I was as relaxed as I wish I had been the first time: I nursed whenever and wherever; I've mastered the messy diaper, and I gave up on "doing it all" at home.

I also focused more on soaking up every ounce of my newborn and toddler, and I put the chores low on my list of priorities.

I have learned how to confidently say no as moth⁻ er. Visitors—friends, family, neighbors, etc.—will want to get their hands on your baby and while I welcomed company, there were times I just had to say no, unapologetically.

CHAPTER

3. Make Arrangements to Pump at Work

"Be firm about your pumping needs—times and location—and get it worked out before you leave, because you'd be surprised how unaccommodating some workplaces are about this."

~ *Betty, age 34, District of Columbia*

The American Academy of Pediatrics (AAP) recom‾mends "exclusive breastfeeding for about the first six months of a baby's life, followed by breastfeeding in combination with the introduction of complementary foods until at least twelve months of age."

But it's very difficult, if not impossible, for a new mother to actually implement these guidelines if she chooses to breastfeed once maternity leave ends and she returns to work. This being the case, I wasn't surprised at how often the topic of breastfeeding and pumping came up in the surveys and interviews I completed.

New working mothers were frustrated for various reasons—some didn't have access to an appropriate facility (e.g., a proper lactation room) but instead had to pump in glorified closets or in empty conference rooms (and use printer paper or scarves to cover the windows in the door).

Other women found themselves stuck in back-to-back meetings all day and found it difficult to step out or block their calendar to pump. The lack of consistent pumping times made it difficult for some women to keep up their milk supply.

In addition, some working moms who needed to pump faced awkward questions regarding why they had to leave early from or arrive late to certain meetings. This is something can I personally attest to, especially on days where I had three or more meetings in a row. I would have to leave one meeting and run to my office to quickly pump and then arrive late to my next meeting.

"If you are going to breastfeed, make sure you have talked to your employer and identified a loca⁻ tion in your place of work in which you can pump breast milk, and be certain you have communicated regarding times you will be allowed to pump. Do this before returning to work."

~ *Laura, age 38, Texas*

"Begin pumping breast milk at home a couple of weeks before you go back, so you know your pump well and are comfortable using it. Make sure your employer provides you time and space to pump if you choose to, talk about it before you go on leave."

~ *Helen, age 41, North Carolina*

"Don't make yourself crazy stashing breast milk— you don't need to fill the freezer. Buy the milk cooler bag and reusable nursing pads. Keep a change of clothes at work in case of leaking or spills."

~ *Jen, age 31, Massachusetts*

Be proactive and start the conversation - you can't just assume that your manager will know that you plan to pump at work. Depending on your comfort level with you manager, I would certainly make sure to establish the fact that you do need a sufficiently clean and private pumping space and will need to be away from your desk periodically. If you feel uncomfortable discussing the issue with a male manager, or you don't have an easy rapport with your manager, then I would suggest addressing issues around pumping access and space with the Human Resources department. They are your best advocates in the workplace.

~ *Tara, HR Manager*

Resource Spotlight: Pumping Tips by Kristine Golden

The following advice is from Kristine Golden, Founder of Milla-Beyond Maternity, which offers business-appropri‾ate, functional clothing for nursing/pumping women.

Going back to work after maternity leave, let alone pumping at work, was difficult. I stressed about my baby in daycare; I stressed about how much baby was eating and wondered how much he might cry or sleep. I also stressed about my performance at work, about commuting, about pumping milk.

If I was going to keep nursing and pumping, I knew I had to make it as easy as I could at work. There are now a record number of American moms who are breastfeeding, but there is a significant drop in breastfeeding rates between six months and one year. I believe one of the reasons is because trying to nurse and pumping at work is hard.

Here are some tips that might help set you up for successful pumping at work.

Invest in a quality pump.

I invested in an electric, closed system, double pump for work. It was important for me that it was a closed system that put a barrier between the milk and the pump tubing. Being able to pump both breasts simultaneously was a huge timesaver. I also bought a manual pump for home, since I nurse on demand and don't often have to pump at home.

Purchase a specialty pumping bra or tank.

There are some great specialty bras from Rumina, Dairy Fairy, and Simple Wishes that you can wear comfortably all day and not have to deal with changing in and out of with a pumping corset. It makes a tremendous difference to have a hands-free pump bra. Don't forget the Bamboobies for when you get a little leaky.

Wear nursing/pumping friendly clothing.

I'm lucky my office has a dedicated space for nurs⁻ ing moms to pump, but my day was made easier when I could simply unzip the front of my dress. Tops and dresses that have a surplice neckline or double-layer make it faster to hook up a pump or to nurse on demand. Companies like Milla—Beyond Maternity, which I founded, Latched Mama, and Figure 8 Maternity offer options at different price points and styles.

Commit to a consistent pumping schedule.

I blocked off three 30-minute breaks each day to pump: 9:00 a.m., 12:00 p.m., and 3:00 p.m. This was critical when I first went back to work to manage being engorged. As time went on, I dropped to two pump sessions (11:00 a.m. and 4:00 p.m.). Sure, some days it was hard to juggle meetings, but federal law states that most employers must provide breaks and a private place to pump.

Steady water intake and a lactation-friendly diet

It's very important to drink a lot of water and eat foods that encourage milk production, such as oat⁻ meal. There are some great oatmeal cookie recipes that double as "lactation cookies."

Every day was a success that I could nurse, and I made time for pumping. The game changers for me were the pump bra and nursing-friendly clothing. That quick access allowed me to cut my pump breaks to between 15-20 minutes. The longer I nursed my baby, the more confident I became, and that helped my milk supply.

CHAPTER

4. Confirm HR + Management Are in Agreement

"My employer completely wiped my employee information from the system because HR didn't communicate with my management that my leave had been extended, nor did my management reach out to me before removing my employee creden⁻ tials."

~ *Kate, age 36, Maryland*

Why is it so important for an expectant mom to coor‐ dinate with her manager and the company's HR and benefits team? Because coordinating maternity leave is usually a cross-functional effort between Human Resources, a benefits department, and management. This can lead to miscommunication, forms not getting filled out in time, supervisors being left out of the loop, etc.

One of the most critical things for expectant moms to do is to manage the process as best as she can. Don't make assumptions about how you think it is going to work. Ask each person, "What do you need from me now? Who should I follow up with?" etc., and then follow those instructions to the T!

Another important task most expectant moms fail to do is to correctly document any discussions around maternity leave policy and, more importantly, make sure all parties—Human Resources, benefits, man‐ agement—are on the same page.

Get Everything in Writing!

If possible, I would recommend either initiating or summarizing maternity leave discussions over email. It's much easier to keep track of who said what over email, and if you have a new manager or need clarifi‐ cation, you can forward emails to HR, etc.

Whether it's a casual conversation or formal meet‐ ing, always follow up with an email confirming the talking points. If you don't want to write something formal, you can simply send an email that says, *"Hey, I want to make sure I heard you right about XXX."*

The purpose is to have a record, not to win points for style. In your emails, write out all the details that you discussed, questions you have, and any follow-ups that need to be done on your end. It helps set expectations and reduce miscommunication.

Documenting your communications will also help you to navigate unforeseen challenges. You don't want to be in a place where you return from work and have a different manager (like me), get into a dispute over something with HR, or find your job has changed, and you are now trying to recall discussions you had several months prior.

"Make sure things are in writing, and approach it as something you are entitled to, not something your employer or manager is doing for you as a favor."

~ *Anne, 33, Connecticut*

"My position was not eligible for official leave. We agreed over email to "work something out" but didn't go into details.

However, the company lost a contract right after my baby was born. I was not given any work but was also not officially fired, either. I found out later that my colleagues thought our manager had laid me off.

It was a weird situation and if I had to do it over again, I would push for a more concrete agreement of what "work something out" meant and gotten the terms in writing.

~ Dana, age 31, Virginia

Mom Spotlight: Janet, Sr. Manager

Janet, Sr. Manager, Management Consulting

I thought work wouldn't be any different when I returned from maternity leave. That I would still be supported and continue on my path in my career. But when I returned, it was a struggle.

Changes at work:

I had laid out a path to promotion prior to taking my maternity leave, all the partners were support⁻ive, so I didn't think much of it.

Then I came back 6 weeks after delivery, wanting to plan out how the rest of my year would go. I got lucky, as they were able to keep me local until my baby was 6 months old, working from home, and then I traveled 3-4 days a week.

I tried to switch divisions into a lower tier of con⁻sulting in an attempt to travel less, but I am now seen as a liability vs. an asset because I have travel limitations. Furthermore, the partners told me there would be no pay cut, and then earlier this year, they said it would be about a 25% cut.

I am still working, but I'm shopping for a job on the side.

What I learned while I was on maternity leave:

I work way too much. As consultants, we travel, and we are always heads-down as we are pretty much on-call all the time. I was stressed and literally didn't even know it.

While I was on leave, I loved being able to wake up and not feel stressed about everything that I needed to get done that day. I could go and meet with other moms and talk about mom-related issues that affected me emotionally, psychologically, etc.

It was nice having that time to recover because it's a huge identity crisis, and everyone kind of expects you to be a normal person when you've literally had another human come out of you.

Not to mention, you go from having disposable time to no time at all, and even if you work from home, there's never enough time to do everything. Even now, I get caught up in it. Working early in the morning at 5:00 a.m., working after my daughter goes to bed, and in the end, I'm just an employee; they don't really care about me.

CHAPTER

5. Start Planning for Childcare Earlier

"Start early! We visited every daycare in between my house and my work when I was two months pregnant, and all of them had waitlists already."

~ *Hallie, age 34, Pennsylvania*

New moms should not be surprised to discover long waitlists—sometimes as long as six months to one year—at some of the more popular childcare facilities. Especially facilities that offer great services at relatively reasonable rates. Therefore, I highly recommend expectant mothers not wait until after the baby arrives before they start looking for reputable centers and lining up childcare.

For moms who plan to go the nanny route, unfortunately, it is not uncommon to spend months searching for and finding the perfect one-on-one caregiver, only for that arrangement to fall through at the last moment.

This is incredibly stressful and leaves a lot of new moms without easy options because many of these moms never considered looking at daycare facilities as a backup option. Similarly, if a family member plans to watch your child, that arrangement can also fall through, so you need to be prepared.

Nanny Share

In the last 2-3 years, I have seen a growing interest in a nanny share, where two or more families share a nanny and split the costs. Sounds wonderful, right? Not so fast. I interviewed several moms who regretted not properly researching or setting clear expectations for the nanny share.

The post, *This is How a Nanny Share Actually Works!*, on NannyCounsel.com is a great read for moms who want to learn more about the advantages (and challenges) of a nanny share.

Tips and Strategies from Other Moms

"Try to use vacation/sick days to make the transi‐ tion back easier for you and your baby. For exam‐ ple, prepare to go back to work, if possible, on a Thursday. The next week, work from Monday through Wednesday, and then take Thursday and Friday off.

~ Laura, age 38, New Jersey

"Research childcare options and facilities well be‐ fore returning to work, as there may be a waiting list. If you aren't going to be able to afford the fees for daycare, many centers offer a childcare subsidy but you need to apply early! It takes time to process and receive the subsidy if you qualify."

~ *Danielle, age 37, Florida*

"Having family help to care for your little one can be really challenging. Set clear boundaries from the get-go and be willing to be okay with things not being perfect. It's a hard balance."

~ *Alison, age 33, Pennsylvania*

Expert Advice: Daycare Centers

For my blog, Philly Baby Bump, I interviewed Tina, a Director of a daycare center in the Philadelphia area, and she offered the following advice:

If you are currently pregnant and thinking of enrolling your child in daycare, you should begin visiting daycare centers now! It is exhausting to visit a center while working and pregnant, so you'll want enough lead time to visit, talk to staff, find out what the day in the life of an infant or toddler is like, etc., without the time pressure of being 8 or 9 months pregnant.

More importantly, as soon as you walk through the door, trust your mommy instinct! In addition to the normal list of questions around certifications, activities, etc., ask yourself, how secure is the building? Can I drop my child off every day and entrust them with my most precious gift ever? Will I be able to focus at work because I know my baby is being loved and cared for?

Lastly, be wary of centers that only let you stop in with an appointment. We believe parents need to see the center as it is and recommend pregnant moms visit us multiple times before enrolling. We even encourage new moms to bring their baby, and visit us for a couple of hours to get to know the staff and ask additional questions that may not have come to mind pre-birth.

Mom Spotlight: Elizabeth, Project Manager

Elizabeth, Project Manager
for an Architecture Firm

My husband and I both wanted to keep our child out of daycare for the first year and then join a nanny share. We thought really hard about our plan, and it was really hard to broach the subject with the office (we work in the same firm).

I was beyond stressed to ask for more than the twelve weeks because another mom was also ask⁻ ing for leave time around my due date. My husband was very adamant about taking leave, too. Most dads at our office take two or three days. He wanted two weeks flat out and then flex-time for the next month, at least.

We work in a very high-pressure field but asked for what we wanted. It felt as if we were asking for the world.

Expectations vs. reality:

I thought I would have the baby, drop by for some meetings once in awhile, then go back to work part time after four or five months. My mom would watch the baby while I was working two or three days a week, and I'd work during naps, etc.

What actually happened was we had a baby, but when it was time to go back, there wasn't enough work for me. I ended up being home about seven months. I started back part time, and my mom watched our son two days a week. We paid her, so there was no guilt or resentment.

We had issues getting pregnant the first time, so we wanted a second child and miraculously got pregnant right away. We interviewed nannies to watch both kids, and it was so expensive we decided to wait another few months. It has now been eighteen months, and we are making arrangements for me to start working part-time this fall.

Childcare advice:

I recommend paying any family members who watch your kids, even if you don't pay them as much as you'd pay a sitter. My mom didn't want to be paid, but it cost her gas money to drive to us, plus wear and tear on her car, etc. We worked it out and paid her $50 a day, and she was thankful for a little spending money.

Finding parent friends:

I found parent friends right away through a parenting class with my eldest, and I am still friends with those parents. Meeting other new moms in the class was pivotal to me feeling like a human again.

CHAPTER

6. Save, Save, Save

"My biggest regret is that I didn't save more mon‐ ey to make my leave longer. I could probably have asked for more unpaid time, but I financially couldn't afford it."

~ Ling, age 35, Pennsylvania

The number one piece of advice the survey and inter‐ view participants gave to expectant or new moms was to *"Save, save, save!"* This wasn't surprising, given the high incidences of unpaid leave. However, many families fail to research and factor in the high cost of childcare, further exacerbating the need to start sav‐ ing well before taking maternity leave.

Talking and thinking about money can be stressful, so parents sometimes ignore this subject. But it's im‐ portant to discuss your finances and plan accordingly.

Expert Advice: Financially Prepare for Maternity Leave

The following advice is from Wilson Muscadin, Founder of The Money Speakeasy, a forum for young professionals to discuss and learn fundamental money-management topics.

When my wife and I started to think about having children, we were excited by the idea, but after some time, the questions (and anxiety) started to kick in:

"Wait, can we even afford to have a child?"
"How much should I save?"
"Does my job even have paid maternity leave?"

There's so much involved with bringing new life into the world, and we really didn't want to add financial stress to the list. We put together the following tips to help you financially prepare for maternity leave.

Evaluate your health insurance coverage, includ⁻ ing in-network services.

Call your health insurance provider and ask what maternity programs or resources they cover. Many insurers offer benefits to assist you from pregnancy to postpartum, which can save you time and a signifi- cant amount of money. Sample benefits include, vouchers or discounts for childbirth education cour- ses, free breast pumps, and up to 6 free visits from a registered dietitian or lactation consultant.

It's also very important to make sure all your healthcare providers are in-network. If you plan to give birth in a hospital, confirm your obstetrician and his or her attending hospitals are in-network. There is nothing worse than getting a $2000 bill for your hos- pital stay that also comes home with you.

Have a written monthly budget.

Whether you have had a written budget before or not, it's time to buckle down and write and stick to a monthly budget. Personally and with clients I've worked with, our perception of our food expendi- tures, for example, and the reality, are typically very different.

When I ask my clients how much they spend on food and then look at their bank statements combin⁻ ing all eating out (coffee, breakfast, lunches, fast food, drinks, restaurants) and grocery shopping, people are spending nearly double what they think.

In our case, even with a budget, we were over-spending our food budget by hundreds of dollars. So just the very process of accounting for *actual* spending can open one's eyes for significant opportunities for savings.

You can also start saving by cutting out non-essential spending, such as cable, eating out, and getting rid of monthly membership fees for services you rarely use or don't really need.

Finally, you will likely have to re-prioritize certain aspects of your finances. For example, if you were making additional payments on your student loans to pay them off quicker, you may want to reallocate that money toward an emergency savings or a baby fund.

Start a "baby fund."

A baby fund is sort of a catchall fund for financial items related to maternity leave and the additional monthly expenses. When my wife and I started thinking about having children, we set aside some money each month to put in the baby fund, including a portion of our bonuses. The purpose of the fund was to protect our monthly cash flow if things became more expensive than we anticipated, which came in handy when we discovered how expensive daycares were in our area.

We didn't start looking into daycare until the middle of the second trimester, and after visiting several daycare facilities, the one we truly wanted was nearly $2000/mo. That was significantly more than we had planned to spend and was even more than our rent at the time. We were adamant about not incurring debt or using credit cards, so the baby fund served as a buffer to help cover the increased childcare expense.

Everyone is different in terms of what makes them comfortable financially, but if, for example, childcare expenses for the first full year average about $12K, that's $1K/mo. Have a discussion with your partner about how increasing your expenses by $1K/mo. would affect your budget and your financial goals. Do a test run by saving $1K/mo. in advance to see what it feels like. Again, for us, daycare itself was significantly more than that, which is why the fund came in handy.

Lean on your village.

Most people have trouble asking for help, but you'll need to lean on others during and after your pregnancy. Financially speaking, baby showers are a great way for the "village" to help you get what you need to prepare for the child's arrival, but be sure to focus your baby registry on needs, not wants.

For example, before we created our baby registry, we spoke to other new moms and received a list of items that were top priority versus nice-to-haves or not needed. Also, we didn't need his baby high chair immediately, but we were glad we put those items on the registry because we didn't have to worry about the cost of getting one down the road.

For those in your village who may not be able to afford more expensive items on a baby registry, dia‾pers, baby clothes, home-cooked meals, and babysitting are great, low-cost substitutes. Allowing people to help and contribute brings them joy and takes some financial burden off of you.

Consider purchasing some items secondhand.

You may have some fairly new parents in your work or social circle who are more than willing to off⁻ load clothes, toys, strollers, and bouncers to you, so don't be afraid to ask. You want to avoid paying retail prices for items that will only be useful for a short time.

There are things that you don't want to purchase secondhand due to safety concerns: cribs, high chairs, car seats, and old strollers. Another benefit of getting secondhand is that some items/toys are adored by some babies and loathed by others.

Don't make the same mistake we did by buying the $100+ bouncer with all the features, only to have our son spend a total of 10 minutes in the bouncer and not liking it at all. Would you know he ended up spending hours upon hours in a simple Fisher Price bouncer, which was gifted to us secondhand by our neighbors?

The lesson was that "features" marketing is geared toward adults; babies are not concerned about fea⁻ tures. Remember that a lot of baby toys and items have short-term usefulness, and your baby may not even like it—so hold on to your money.

Resource Spotlight: Take 12 Maternity Registry

The following interview features Margi Scott, Founder of Take 12, a maternity leave registry that allows mothers to fundraise for the 12 weeks of FMLA leave.

What was the inspiration behind Take 12?

When preparing for the birth of my twins, I planned to save for my maternity leave, as I had for my other two pregnancies. I did the math and added up what I would need to save to take the full 12 weeks of unpaid FMLA that I qualified for and realized the number was huge. I was further along in my career, and as the breadwinner, my family relied on me for that income more than they had in the past.

To make matters worse, my husband was laid off in the last trimester of my pregnancy, and I ended up delivering five and a half weeks early, which resulted in an emergency C-section, giving me even less time to plan. After a week in the hospital for my own recovery, I had to begin commuting back and forth to the hospital to spend time with my babies, as they were in the NICU for 2 weeks due to premature birth.

One night at the dinner table with my friend and my mom, after an emotional day at the NICU, I did the math surrounding my leave, compounded with the hospital bills I would soon face and the fact that my 12 weeks were ticking away with my babies still in the hospital, and I was totally defeated.

My mother suggested I start a crowd-funding page for my situation, but I didn't feel right with that, knowing that my situation was not unique to what most women face.

The thought intrigued me, though, and I hopped online to do some research on "maternity leave and crowdfunding," only to find over 2,000 women who had already turned to crowdfunding to fund their maternity leave! I realized the need—it's socially acceptable for us to ask for stuff in the form of a baby registry, so why can't we ask for the time we really need? That's how Take 12 was born.

What advice would you give to mothers that are hesitant about registering?

Friends, family, and close co-workers really do want to help new moms, but they simply don't know how to help, aside from buying a gift. Take 12 is for every expecting mom—even those who don't feel they need the financial support—as it allows them to make a statement saying, "I value the time I need with my baby above all else; here's how you can help."

If expectant moms are interested, what should they think through before registering?

There is a page on our website that walks our moms through the mathematical steps of determining how much you must financially plan for in order to take your full leave. This is something everyone must consider and take time to decipher, as the financial strain of taking full leave can be greater than most moms—especially first-time moms—think.

Second, speak from the heart when you are writing your story. Tell your friends and family the truth about your excitement and worry. The people in your life care about your experience, and they want to be a part of it. We also feature an option for adoptive par-ents and will be launching Take 12 Dads in spring/summer 2017. For more info, www.mytake12.com

Part II: My Story

CHAPTER

7. Returning to Work

On August 6, one week before I was supposed to re‐ turn back to work after being on maternity leave, I received the following text:

First, a Little Background

The text was from my co-worker (we will call her "Laura"). Laura was sharing news from my/our manager, ("Dan"). Before I get into how I felt about receiving that text message and what it all meant, allow me to give you a bit of background...

About three months into my pregnancy, I had received a promotion into a new role that involved taking over a component of Laura's responsibilities. The day I received the promotion was also the day I reached the twelve-week pregnancy milestone, so I let HR know I was pregnant shortly after they delivered the news about my promotion.

I researched my company's maternity leave policy shortly after announcing my pregnancy and made a maternity leave plan. Based on my role, my work experience, the company policy, etc., I was going to take a total of fourteen weeks of maternity leave. That broke down as follows:

• Three weeks short-term disability, paid at 100% of my salary.
• Three weeks short-term disability, paid at 50% of my salary.
• Four weeks of vacation/paid time off (PTO).
• Four weeks of unpaid leave.

To prepare financially, I left my annual bonus untouched to cover my four weeks of unpaid leave. As far as work, my promotion meant I would be taking over an aspect of Laura's job that she had been doing for years. It was decided that Laura would continue to perform this role over the summer while I was on leave, and then I would resume the position full-time, taking over one hundred percent of those duties upon my return to work.

When I put together my maternity leave plan, I, among many things, broke down each of my fourteen weeks' time off and listed:

• How that week would be covered (for example, STD, vacation, unpaid, etc.)
• My due date.
• When I planned on returning to work.
• My transition plan for coming back, which in⁻ cluded working from home for the first two weeks, then working from home two days a week for one month, and finally, working from home one day a month for the remainder of the calendar year (which was about three months).

My manager Dan was completely fine with the arrangement and didn't have any objections. He said, "Whatever you need, just send me an email with the details, and make sure to CC Human Resources so they know I'm okay with it." The entire discussion lasted less than 5 minutes. His response was incredible and made me feel wonderful about not having to fight for anything.

On my last day of work, I was so very excited and ready to give birth. I'd grown physically uncomfort⁻ able, and the anticipation was overwhelming. I was so excited to finally see my baby!

The birth was wonderful—no complications—and we came home filled with so much love for our daughter. We were anxious to start our journey as a family, but man, postpartum life was ridiculously hard. Those first weeks were all a blur—I think I sleepwalked through a routine of the baby waking up, eating, and going to sleep every two to three hours, twenty-four hours a day, seven days a week. My husband and I were completely exhausted, but those weeks away from work and focusing on my baby were amazing.

My husband is an academic professor, and our daughter's May birth meant that we were able to spend the entire summer together. I realized then but even more so now how fortunate the timing was. While both of our parents stopped by to visit the baby, we did not ask anyone else to help take care of her. It was just us and while difficult, we really bonded as a new family right away.

Changes at Work

Now that you have the background, allow me to return to that text message. As soon I received that text—again, a week before I was supposed to return to work—I showed it to my husband, and he said, "Uh-oh, that can't be good."

Two hours later, I had managed to work up the courage to phone Laura back. And about the change "that will be good for both of us"? Well, I would now be reporting to Laura, not to Dan. This might seem trivial, but in the corporate world, the old saying, "people leave managers, not companies" is especially true.

To say I was unhappy would be a gross under-statement. I strongly believe a person's manager directly determines how much they will like their job, and if I had known I would be reporting to Laura, I never would have accepted the promotion.

Laura was a micromanager who was overly focused on minutiae, and I was allergic to that style of leadership. Knowing this, I also had a moment where I realized that I was never going to take over the responsibilities that were part of the role I had accepted.

But what choice did I have? I was a new mom; I was already struggling with all the challenges that come with motherhood. I hated my body, I was hormonal, and I was mentally and physically exhausted. I didn't have it in me to fight another battle at the time, so I decided to "agree" with the new arrangement and wait it out.

But the situation only grew worse. Even though Dan had easily approved my work-from-home arrangement, Laura made it clear she was not a fan. She told me, "Dan doesn't allow work-from-home schedules." I knew this was false, as there were other people on his team who worked from home once a week, not to mention the fact that Dan had easily approved my arrangements, and it hadn't affected my working relationship with him. Laura would also make comments such as, "I worked when I was on *my* maternity leave."

I didn't want to complain to Dan because he was a senior executive, and I felt as if I needed to handle it myself. I debated whether to argue with Laura, but then I realized I had CC'd HR about my maternity leave and transition plan back to work, which included working from home.

That gave me the confidence to stand my ground and mention to Laura that HR knew about the agreement. It was stressful and awkward, but I was so glad that per Doug's suggestion, I had notified HR ahead of time. I am not confident that I would have been able to keep that arrangement if I had not done that.

My Blog - Philly Baby Bump

While all of the drama was going on at work, I was running a little blog—*Philly Baby Bump*—on the side. It all started when I was in my second trimester of pregnancy. I was looking for a local, prenatal yoga class and noticed there weren't too many Philadelphia websites or blogs dedicated to pregnant women.

I found a lot of mom blogs that listed local activi¯ties for young children or family-oriented events, but none of the sites seemed to reach out to expecting moms or moms with children under age two. I thought it was silly that the 5th largest city in the U.S.A. didn't have a website tailored to pregnant women, so I decided to start my own.

I didn't know how to go about this, but I knew that if I was looking for prenatal information in Philly, other people were, too. Once I began exploring how to create a blog, I discovered there was *tons* of free information on how to get started, and my journey be¯gan.

At the time, I had no great ambition to turn *Philly Baby Bump* into a full-time, income-generating blog— heck, I wasn't even a big blog reader back then—I just figured, why not? I was under a lot of stress from my day job, my daughter was in bed by 7:00 p.m. most nights (although she still woke up every few hours), and I needed an outlet. I wanted something that was all mine.

I'd work on the blog in the evenings and on week⁻ ends. Although it was sometimes exhausting, I was used to working long, demanding hours in my previ- ous careers, so I could handle it.

Besides, I was motivated by my newly discovered love of creating something that didn't require the use of Microsoft Excel or PowerPoint! Even better, I was talking to and meeting with all types of inspiring women and mothers in Philadelphia, and many of them were in the maternity services industry. People were actually visiting my blog and reading my posts. It was all so strange because it was completely new territory for me, but I loved every moment!

I also loved that I didn't have to deal with point⁻ less meetings and bureaucracy when working on my blog. I didn't have to seek approval, and looking back, I realize I was probably rebelling against being suffocated and micromanaged in my full-time role.

CHAPTER

8. Taking the Leap

About ten months in, the situation at work had grown even tenser, and I was simultaneously drained by the time I got home to do my "second shift." My husband is wonderful, but it shouldn't come as a surprise that working mothers still bear a greater burden of the childrearing and household tasks (this statement is supported by multiple research reports).

I would leave work around 4:00 p.m. and then rush home to play with my daughter while talking to the nanny about my daughter's day. I would then log back into my computer to finish up a couple of work-related items, get dinner ready, and then play with my daughter again before feeding her, bathing her, and getting her ready for bed. My husband came home around 6:30 p.m., and given that our daughter went to bed so early, it was hard for him to do a lot of these tasks during the weekdays.

I began to notice that I wasn't as present mentally when I was with my daughter. I was often mulling over my bad day at work or thinking about follow-up tasks from a meeting.

I was stressed, frustrated, and angry that my manager and role had changed without me having any say in the decision-making process. I felt stuck and marginalized in my role, and I was also struggling with leaving my daughter with a wonderful but expensive nanny, while I went to a job I hated. Was it really worth the salary if I was this unhappy?

The Final Straw

The final straw—which occurred approximately one year before I began writing this book—came about when I had a one-on-one meeting with Laura. We were having a disagreement about a work assignment I had done. She said—and I'll never forget it—"Victoria, I know you're smart and ambitious, but frankly, I'm not really sure what your capabilities are."

At that moment, the world kind of stopped. I don't mean to be dramatic, but that is the only way I can explain it. For one thing, I couldn't believe someone— let alone my manager—had just said that to me. I was sort of internally devastated. I was angry. I was furious. I was humiliated. I was all of these things, and all within a matter of seconds. I don't think I replied or said anything for a minute or more. I actually don't even know how I responded, verbatim, but I said something along the lines of, "I think we'll just have to continue this discussion at another time. If you don't know what my capabilities are, then I'm not really sure what I'm doing here."

I got up and left her office. I managed to walk out stoically, but I barely made it to my office down the hall before I burst into tears and started crying—like, ugly, sobbing, dry-heaving crying. I even wrote down what she had said, word for word, because I had a feeling I wasn't going to remember if I didn't. Luckily, it was late in the afternoon, so there weren't many people on our floor who could hear me (at least I don't think so).

That was the first time I had ever cried at work. I'd always considered myself pretty "anti-crying at work", and yet, there I was, sitting in my chair, sobbing. After a couple of minutes, I managed to pull myself together enough to call my husband and tell him what happened. I then left work, went home, had a huge glass of red wine, and tried to calm down… and a week later, I resigned.

Part of what made resigning easier was that contrary to what my manager had said, I *knew* I had several capabilities, and the blog was just one example of what I could do with my talents. While I wasn't making an income anywhere close to my old, full-time salary, my blog did make a few hundred dollars a month. I knew I was onto something, and I just needed the freedom to explore.

CHAPTER 8 - TAKING THE LEAP

The company I worked for was wonderful and supportive in my decision to leave, and I will be forever grateful for the relationships I developed there. I could have stayed if I had wanted to, taken on a different role, but the damage had been done. I didn't have a backup plan, but I knew I needed to be home, taking care of my daughter and taking the leap into a new phase of life that involved figuring out *my* purpose in life.

I say leap because a few weeks before my resignation, I knew I needed to change my work situation, but I didn't know what that meant. Frankly, I was afraid to take a step into the unknown.

The fear was holding me back, but then a girlfriend of mine shared the Steve Harvey *Jump* video, which you can easily find on YouTube.

I have often heard the same message throughout my life—so much so that it has almost become a cliché. I mean, who hasn't, right? You have a couple of cocktails, dream big for a little bit, and then go to bed and wake up for work the next day. But this time was different. Something clicked when I watched that video, and after the fateful incident with my manager, I knew I needed to just *Jump*, and go for it.

I also made the choice to never, ever be in a position where I would allow someone to talk to me like that again, to never allow myself to feel powerless, and to never give that type of power to anyone. I knew I was smart, hard working, creative, and ultimately, I had a feeling that I was going to be okay. Call it faith, call it instinct—I just knew I had to trust that feeling.

The following was taken from part of my blog post called, *Why I Left My Job to Become a Stay-at-Home Mom.*

"The fear is still strong and very present. Because really, how the heck am I going to make money?!

But if I have to do multiple lower-paying freelancing jobs that allow me to work from home, eat peanut butter and jelly sandwiches for dinner, and cut back significantly on all things good (including my beloved wine), it will still be worth it.

Even two weeks removed from my full-time job, I feel like I am really getting to know my daughter in a different way. While some would say that's because I'm spending more time with her, I don't think it's that simple. I actually think it's because I am more present when I am spending time with her.

Not having distractions from a job that I came to dislike has freed up so much mental space. Will it always be like this? Probably not, but for now I am enjoying getting to be with her as she takes her first steps and becomes a beautiful little person.

I really want to emphasize that making this move was not at all easy.

I straddle the world of being a business professional that has an MBA from a top school and has worked at some of the most prestigious corporations with also being an immigrant whose Kenyan mother tirelessly worked 2-3 jobs when I was growing up (including overnight and weekend shifts). My mother is such an incredible source of inspiration to me and I worry leaving corporate America may seem indulgent.

Because let's be REAL:

Bills are REAL.

Student loan debt is REAL.

Leaving a high-profile job with a six-figure salary is REAL.

But for me, this is something I have to do. I NEED to do. If I don't, I will regret it and I can't live my life like that. Whether I fail or succeed, at least it's my authentic journey.

Until then, it's time for a lot of prayers and peanut butter and jelly sandwiches!

The Aftermath

Since that post almost one year ago, life has changed indeed. Practically speaking, my lifestyle has changed pretty dramatically since my income is not at the level it was (at least for now). However, the trade-offs have easily made it worth it. It has been easy to stop spending money on expensive clothes, vacations, happy hours, and meals out when the benefit is me waking up every morning feeling present, alive, and soaking in so much new knowledge.

Shawn Achor, a Harvard psychologist says, "Happiness is the joy you feel striving toward your potential." I experience that every single day, even when the ups and downs of being a mom, wife, and entrepreneur get me frustrated.

My blog has allowed me to both use my business background and get in touch with my creative side. I get to meet inspiring women who are balancing motherhood with their passions and businesses. Most importantly, I am learning who I am, outside of the career I had worked so hard to establish myself in. I'm no longer that woman who is waiting for that new title, promotion, or annual performance review to dictate my worth.

Looking back, I wouldn't change anything that happened. If I had gone back into the role I had expected when I went on maternity leave with no change in managers, I know I would still be in the corporate world, making really good money (which I admit I definitely miss!), but I would have never fulfilled this part of me that I never knew was there.

Motherhood fundamentally changed me. I thought I had it all figured out and that a baby meant more coffee and more patience, not a complete life change and a whole new way of thinking. I am a pretty confident person most of the time, but becoming a mother gave me an internal sense of strength and confidence to trust myself as a person, rather than to trust in my resume.

The stories in the next section discuss unexpected career challenges that expectant mothers may face as they prepare to return to work.

Part III: I Didn't Expect To...

CHAPTER

9. Start Searching For a New Job

"Before your child is born, start looking for alternative jobs in case something goes wrong. I found myself out of work for much longer than I expected and regret that I didn't have didn't have other options in place. It was a huge hit to our family's finances and to my sense of myself.

~ *Rebecca, age 34, New Jersey*

While researching for this book, I encountered several women who wish they had given more thought to looking for new jobs prior to taking maternity leave. The reasons varied: some mothers wanted a more "family-friendly" role, some wanted to take a longer maternity leave than their employers were willing to give, others had difficulty transitioning back to work and felt their team or manager wasn't supportive, and some unfortunate moms did not have a job to come back to.

Whatever your reason, I encourage you to at least explore your options, and take a look at some of the fantastic companies and resources featured in this chapter. As I mentioned earlier, I didn't receive any form of compensation for featuring the experts, ser⁻ vices, products, etc. mentioned in this book. These are all resources that I have either personally used, found through my research, or were referred to me through reputable sources.

> "When someone from my workplace went on ma⁻ ternity leave, the rest of the team members were often less than supportive. I'd been back to work about a month, and I had asked for some vacation time I had already earned. I got a lecture from a manager that my coworkers were at a disadvantage because I had been out on leave. I was pretty mad about this talk, but I took the time anyway and then started looking for a new job."

> ~ *Ling, age 35, Pennsylvania*

THE INSIDER'S GUIDE TO MATERNITY LEAVE

Resource Spotlight: Fairygodboss

The following interview features Romy Newman, Co-Founder of Fairygodboss, a website designed to help professional women get the inside scoop on maternity leave policies, pay, corporate culture, benefits and work flexibility.

What was the inspiration for Fairygodboss?

My co-founder Georgene Huang and I worked together at Dow Jones, the parent company of the Wall Street Journal. One day, there was a very sudden management shake-up—and Georgene was fired out of nowhere. To make matters worse, she was 2 months pregnant. And had a one-year old at home.

No one did anything wrong in firing Georgene. But it made her realize that there were some very important things she'd want to know about her next employer before she even interviewed.

There are many tools out there these days, such as Payscale, Glassdoor, and Indeed, that collect crowd-sourced information about companies and job reviews. But Georgene felt as if those sites were very male-dominated. Instead of finding a job, Georgene started experimenting with building Fairygodboss. She wanted to see if there was a real appetite for this information. And she and I reconnected.

I was at a juncture, too. I loved my job at The Wall Street Journal, but I was feeling stuck. I felt as if corporate life did not afford me the flexibility I wanted to spend time with my kids—especially while they were still little/preschool age. I was also tired of the limitations of the corporate structure. So I eagerly came over to join Georgene.

Now almost two years later, hundreds of thousands of women are visiting Fairygodboss to find career advice and seek information about companies and jobs. We're so proud of the traction we've seen!

What advice do you have for an expectant mom who is thinking about changing jobs or careers?

Do not be deterred by a new baby. There are so many opportunities to research jobs and companies online, and I am a huge proponent of ongoing networking. At all points in your career, you should always be networking and building relationships with people outside your current company and industry.

At the same time, I also advise that you can and should definitely window-shop for a new career or job before you go out on maternity leave. But you shouldn't make commitments.

It's really difficult to anticipate how you'll feel after having a baby, and each person experiences it differently. My personal experience was that when I had my son, I felt strongly that it was not the time to ramp up my career. Instead, I wanted to take a step back for a short while.

That said, I know another mom who used the second half of her maternity leave to job search and interview full force, and she found an exciting new job that she was very happy to land.

What sections on Fairygodboss.com should expectant moms visit to explore new jobs or get career advice?

Job reviews for women by women. You can search any company and determine what women have said about how women are treated there, and what kinds of policies, programs, and benefits are available for women.

Maternity leave database. Find out what maternity leave policies are offered by over 2000 companies in the U.S. Find one with a better policy than yours has, and go work there.

Discussion board. This is my favorite area of the site. Users can post about challenges they're facing in the workplace and crowdsource answers from our community.

Maternity leave resources page. Visit this page to find out what your legal rights are and how best to approach maternity leave.

Jobs pages. Thousands of jobs that care about women and gender diversity have posted challenging, exciting and female-friendly jobs to our site.

Expert Advice: Choosing a New Employer

*I interviewed a New York City-based employment attor-
ney, and here are some tips that she provided about
choosing an employer.*

Investigate companies for parent-friendly work-places.

Different organizations compile lists of parent-
friendly / women-friendly workplaces and provide
insight into what the specific policies are at different
companies. Although a policy may say one thing, one
question to explore is what percentage of parents actually take leave? For how long?

One thing that is quite common, unfortunately, is
that a company will give parental leave, but the corporate culture dictates that they should not take the
full leave they may be entitled to.

Talk candidly to current or former employees, ideal-ly parents.

Other parents are a tremendous resource. Find the
parent networks and social media groups where you
can speak candidly regarding how parent friendly a
workplace is. In addition to leave issues, it's important to also investigate other parent-friendly policies,
such as flexible working hours, work-from-home options, company-sponsored or company-subsidized
childcare, child tuition credit, etc. If your child has a

sports game or school show, can you be there without suffering repercussions (formally or informally)?

Ask yourself some hard questions.

What do you need to succeed in the workplace and at home? What type of hours can you expect to work? Are you comfortable with traveling after your child is born? If so, how much? Can your partner or other family and friends be helpful in any way?

Be a smart researcher.

Be careful about who you are telling what information to. Unfortunately, there is a stigma regarding parents in the workplace—women, in particular—that still exists. Asking too many questions about leave and flexibility to the wrong people may signal that you are not serious.

Resource Spotlight: FlexJobs

The following interview features Sara Sutton Fell, CEO of FlexJobs, an employment website that features professional, legitimate jobs that offer some kind of flexibility—telecommuting, part-time or flextime.

Why is FlexJobs.com an ideal job board for new or expectant moms?

FlexJobs is a great job board for new or expectant moms—and all professionals—for a number of reasons! Essentially, every job on our site is a job that fits your life, whether you are looking for a full-time job, a part-time job, or something in between. We focus exclusively on professional-level jobs that offer flexible work options, such as being able to work from home or have a flexible schedule or work part-time or work on freelance projects.

We hear from a lot of new moms who are looking for a flexible job—sometimes, because they are going to stay home with their kids, and they want a way to find part-time position or side jobs to add to the family budget. Or sometimes, because she wants to work full-time, but her current job doesn't offer flexibility. Whatever the reason, the jobs we have on the site can fill these needs—the positions range in experience from entry-level to executive, and we have over 50 career fields to search in.

*You started FlexJobs when you were 7 months preg-
nant with your first child; can you share a little bit
more about that experience?*

I'd been laid off from a high-level position in my
third trimester and was searching for a job. Needless
to say, job searching while you're 7 months pregnant
is…difficult. It was perhaps the first time I really felt
like, as an ambitious woman professional, I was
bumping up against the glass ceiling.

I was looking for a career-oriented position that
offered flexibility as I grew my family, and I was frustrated with having to sift through all the scams, ads,
and junk listings out there. I thought there should be
one place for legitimate, professional-level, flexible
jobs, and that's where the idea for FlexJobs came
from.

*What advice would you give to other expectant moms
who are thinking of starting their own full or part
time business?*

There will always be things in your life that make
starting a new business challenging. But being very
pregnant and then being a new mom as I started this
business definitely made for less-than-ideal timing.

My advice for others is to trust your instincts, and
follow your gut. For me, the idea of FlexJobs was one
I just couldn't stop thinking about. The more I
thought about it, the more it made sense to me. And
so I felt compelled to act on it. If you have that kind of
idea, the kind you just can't shake out of your head,

you might find you can make great things happen, even in less-than-ideal circumstances.

What are some common myths or misconceptions about flexible or telecommunication roles?

One of the biggest is that most telecommuting jobs are for tech-related fields, or that they are telemarket‾ing types of jobs. But that's far from true. We see a huge variety of telecommuting jobs in fields such as medical and health, administrative, sales, customer service, computer & IT, education & training, account-ing & finance, and many other fields.

If you think there won't be telecommuting jobs for your particular career field or career interests, I'm happy to report that there are far more opportunities than people typically imagine!

Do you have only tips for new moms considering a flexible arrangement?

It's important to really think about the type of flex‾ibility that will be most important for you. For some, it's the ability to work from home. For others, it's hav-ing a flexible schedule.

Decide what your priorities are for flexibility—and whether you'd like to work full-time, part-time, or on a project-by-project basis. Knowing this ahead of time will help you focus your job search and find flexible work that truly works for your life.

Resource Spotlight: The Mom Project

The following interview features Alison Robinson, Founder + CEO of The Mom Project, a digital talent marketplace that connects professionally women and stay-at-home moms with career opportunities.

What was the inspiration for The Mom Project

I started The Mom Project while I was on my own maternity leave after having my son, Asher. After becoming a mom, I realized how many sacrifices women have to make while raising a family and managing a full-time career. And I found that according to a Harvard Business Review study, "43% of highly qualified women with children are leaving careers or off-ramping for a period of time."

What was really interesting to me was of those women who left the workforce, many would have kept working if they had access to flexible opportunities. I saw a significant opportunity to create a marketplace that connects talented women seeking flexible opportunities with companies that are committed to building diverse and inclusive organizations.

What are the qualifications and process to join?

Candidates must have an undergraduate degree and five years of professional experience. The Mom Project is equal opportunity, so eligible men can join, too! The process:

1. *Sign Up.* Create your digital profile. Tell us about your education, professional background, and what kinds of opportunities and work arrangements you're interested in.
2. *Participate* - Welcome to our community! Share your Mom Project journey with friends & colleagues.
3. *Get Matched.* We receive new roles across the country each day; a member of our talent team will reach out to you directly as relevant opportunities arise.
4. *Embark.* Find an opportunity you love? Agree to the work scope and details through our digital platform.
5. *Succeed.* Receive compensation and appreciation for a (meaningful) job well done!

What types of work opportunities do you offer?

The Mom Project specializes in four core professional functions: Marketing/PR/Communications, Technology, Human Resources, Finance.

We understand flexibility is not a one-size-fits-all approach and we have a match science that allows us to closely to find the right fit for our talent and employer partners; work types range from 100% remote project based roles to full-time on-site opportunities.

• Project Based - Short term projects
• Maternityship™ - Cover for another parent's maternity leave.
• Permanent Staffing - Part or full time roles

Mom Spotlight: Alison, Oncology Social Worker

Alison, Oncology Social Worker

The morning of my due date, I started having mild contractions, and my husband and I went in for my 40-week check-up. My doctor confirmed that I was in labor and would probably deliver within the next 48 hours. I was so excited to meet my baby and could have easily just called in to my boss to say I was in labor and officially going on leave, but I felt really anxious about taking care of everything at my job.

I actually went into work while my husband went home to get our hospital bag packed. I wanted to make sure I had set up all my away messages, left my desk tidy, and signed off with everyone, as well as run a few errands around the neighborhood.

Returning to work:

I always thought being a working mom would be challenging, but of course, I would want to go back to work. I love my job and was anxious about what it would be like to not work for an extended period of time.

When I was home on leave, I found that was sud‐ denly not true. I loved being with my baby and re‐ ally wanted a full year leave (but only took four and a half months, for which I was incredibly grateful).

All of my priorities shifted, and I just wanted more time with my baby and my family. I never stay late at work anymore and have become so much more efficient, so I can get out the door and home to my family at the end of the day.

Maternity leave:

My due date was in June, and I was certain I was going to have the most amazing summer off. I knew it was going to be work, but it was still a summer off! I'd quickly lose the pregnancy weight as I toted my baby on long walks, get-togethers at local beer gardens, and even head to the beach often.

We didn't get to the beach, and the one time we went to a beer garden, my little one cried the entire time. But we did enjoy so many long walks, which I absolutely loved, a few mommy and me yoga classes at the studio where I had practiced prenatal yoga, and together we checked out every coffee shop in the neighborhood. Each day was exhausting but so gratifying.

It wasn't summer vacation—being a new mom is serious work—but it was the best job I had ever had.

CHAPTER

10. Become a Stay-at-Home Mom

"I took my paid maternity leave but then decided that I wanted to continue staying home, and I quit. If I could have had 5-6 months home, I would have gone back to work, but I only had 2-3 months."

~ *Joyce, age 39, Connecticut*

Many of the mothers that I interviewed and surveyed for this book decided not to return to work after maternity leave. For some, the decision had been made prior to going on leave; for others, it was an unexpected decision, either due to issues at work or unforeseen life circumstances.

Whatever your situation is, think about potential scenarios now, while you are pregnant, so that you can make a more informed decision about the range of feelings you may experience once the baby arrives. What if you don't want to return to work?

I personally remember thinking that I would never be a stay-at-home mom, and yet I was dreading going back to work. You just never know.

"I did not go back to work. I wanted more time off with my baby, and my employer would not hold my position. Be prepared to maybe not go back to work."

~ *Mary, age 34, North Carolina*

"I cried at the thought of leaving my baby with anyone. I just couldn't do it. So my husband & I decided I did not have to go back. Luckily, we were prepared for that financially. Most moms are not, and it's heartbreaking."

~ *Rachel, age 35, Pennsylvania*

Mom Spotlight: Katie, Sr. Manager

Katie, Sr. Manager for Digital Advertising Firm

I never thought I would be a stay-at-home mom—never. Over the course of the first few months, I slowly came to terms with my new identity and priorities and began to build a new vision for my life.

Maternity leave expectations:

I thought I would have a good amount of free time on my maternity leave (I heard newborns sleep constantly), and my main goal for that free time was to search for and land a new job.

My job at the time wasn't very family friendly in a few ways, so I was hoping to find a better role. My plan was to do the research, apply, and interview, all while I was on maternity leave, so I could start working at the new job along the same timeline when my son was 3 months old. Whether going back to my old job or starting a new job, I had planned to be back to work after 3 months.

Reality check:

What actually happened? The early days—the first few months—were just way more intense than I expected. I was not at all mentally or emotionally prepared for the sleep deprivation and no free time. My son ate every 2 hours for almost 9 weeks, so I was a complete zombie. He also had reflux (lots of crying), a milk protein allergy, and eczema.

I didn't want to return to my previous job, and I hadn't started a new job search as originally planned, so my husband and I decided I would leave my job and take a few more months to stabilize and search for a new position.

I wish I had never planned to search for and land a new job while on maternity leave. That was totally unrealistic for me, and it hung over my head and weighed on me. I was already so tired, and it only made me feel more overwhelmed because I was failing at something I had planned to accomplish. If I could do it over again, I would give myself the initial 3 months to just care for my baby and adjust to being a mom.

Biggest regret:

My son has always had a tough time with naps during the day, and I spent sooooo much time try¯ ing to train him to sleep longer. Nothing ever worked, and, after my own research and guidance from my pediatrician, I have just learned to go with the flow on it. I wish I had accepted his unique rhythms earlier because it would have saved me a lot of energy and frustration.

Mom Advice: Tips for a New Stay-at-Home Mom

The following interview features Sarah, a Stay-at-Home Mom (SAHM) from Pennsylvania.

My husband and I planned for me to be a stay-at-home mom, but the transition isn't as easy as some expectant moms may think. The following are some tips that may make your transition a bit easier if you decided to not return to work.

Get out of the house.

Becoming a stay at home mom can be very isolat‾ing, so you want to try to get out of the house often. Even if you don't hang out with other people, go to the mall and walk, go to a park and walk, or just go where other people are. The most important thing is to give yourself a change of scenery to break up the monotony.

Limit use of social media.

It may seem counterintuitive, especially if you don't live close to your family or friends, but sitting on Facebook all day and watching what everyone else is doing gets really depressing.

While it's super fun to post photos and videos of your super cute little one (and get all the likes and loves in response), social media can also make you feel more isolated because of the awareness that you're not interacting in "real life."

Find activities that keep you mentally engaged.

I have a lot of creative hobbies, so I try to spend a lot of time doing those to keep me mentally engaged. For example, I love to cook and bake, so having more time at home gives me the opportunity to try new recipes and learn new skills. I also enjoy knitting while listening to podcasts or audiobooks.

Another thing to try are online classes at a community college. Generally, local community colleges are very low-cost, and it can be fun to take classes just for personal interest.

Find and meet other moms.

I started with the Meet-Up app and found moms' groups in my area. When my little guy was very small, I found that some of the playdates didn't make sense for him because he wasn't mobile, but it was still nice to go anyway and just hang out with the moms.

Also, try to find an exercise group for moms. I started going to mom-based fitness classes when my son was about 3 months old, and not only did I work off my 60 pounds of pregnancy weight gain, but I made several new close friends and built up a great support system.

Expect some conflict...nothing is perfect.

I still find myself having to advocate my value. My husband and I decided together that I would stay home with our son, but there have been more times than I would like to acknowledge that he has voiced that my contribution is less because I'm not making money. I know my husband loves me, and he values what I do, but it is also really easy to think of value only in terms of money—especially since that is what our society emphasizes.

On the other hand, I have learned how to be less hard on myself, and I have learned how to advocate more for myself. It's okay if my home isn't spotless. It's okay if my son is in his pajamas until 3:00 p.m. sometimes. (Heck, it's okay if I'm in my PJs until 3:00 p.m. sometimes!) It's okay if I ate too many cookies today, or skipped my workout yesterday.

I am not perfect, and that's okay. I work hard, I do a good job, and I deserve a break and a day off some‐ times.

Mom Spotlight: Stevie, Sr. Account Executive

Stevie, Sr. Account Executive for
Employee Insurance Benefits Company

I love being a mom and being with my son, but being a full-time, stay-at-home mom is not my calling. My husband, however, is a natural. He is a stay-at-home dad now, and it works perfectly for us.

Expectations vs. reality:

I thought maternity leave would be relaxing and easy, and I'd get to catch up on some sleep that I had been sorely missing in my last trimester. Well, I thought wrong! It was a ton of cleaning up and washing laundry. It was breast milk all over my clothes, it was spit up in my hair, and it was sore nipples and tears. It was work.

Best memory:

One of my best memories from maternity leave included watching my husband learn how to care for a newborn. He was so nervous, and we went through baby care step by step, one thing at a time. He is now the fastest diaper changer this side of the Mississippi and can swaddle a newborn tighter than the burrito I ate for lunch.

CHAPTER

11. Start My Own Business

"It's arguably never the right time start your own business, but if you have the drive and passion - go for it! Find mentors and advisors that push you and can make up for your areas of weakness and never forget to make time for what's important to you - family or otherwise.

~ *Allison Robinson, Founder and CEO of The Mom Project*

Whether it is out of necessity or inspiration or a little bit of both, many first-time expectant moms start their own full or part-time businesses after birth. Some decide to be full-time entrepreneurs, but most of the women I spoke to work full-time outside of the home or are stay-at-home moms, and then they use the early mornings, late nights, and weekends to work on their businesses.

Some stay-at-homes decide to start a side business to generate income and have an outlet or interest out⁻ side of being a mother. Personally speaking, I believe being a stay-at-home mom is at times incredibly lonely (especially in the winter), and if I didn't have my own creative outlet, I would go nuts.

When I started interviewing a lot of women busi⁻ ness owners in the maternity industry for my blog (e.g., doulas, childbirth educations, maternity photographers, etc.), I noticed the same story emerging every time.

Most of these women wanted more flexibility to raise their children or didn't want to return to work, so they started their own businesses. Almost none were what you would call serial entrepreneurs, and for most, it was their first business.

One Approach to Generating Business Ideas

So where to start if you decide you don't want to return to work but need an income, or you are in⁻ spired to do something different? Well, when a new mom and fellow MBA classmate recently said to me,

"I dream about launching a business on my own but can't figure out what or how. This is hard!"

I gave my classmate the following advice, but to be clear, there are many approaches, techniques, and books that try to answer this same problem. In fact, there is a whole aisle of books dedicated to answering this problem, so I don't claim to be an expert.

However, I can only speak to what has worked for me and what I have learned from some of my favorite books and resources as well as from other new moms who are now running successful businesses.

Forget passion, and focus on problems.

"Follow your passion" is great advice if you have one, but I didn't have any and in many ways still don't have one. I mean, who doesn't love traveling and yoga and all of these other things people say when this passion thing comes up? But I don't have one.

I was in investment banking out of undergrad, then I was a bartender and scuba diver instructor for a short period (we will call that my quarter-life crisis), then a management consultant out of business school, and now I'm a mom with a blog, who also decided to write this book.

From that, I think it's pretty clear that I don't have a passion, but I do enjoy learning and trying new things, especially now that I have more freedom to pursue what interests me.

All of this is to say that answering the passion question can be paralyzing for people like me, but what has worked (at least for me) is thinking in terms of solving problems. The activity below always sparks my creativity when I'm not sure what to do.

Try answering and documenting the following questions over a week, and see what you come up with.

• What types of services, products, or daily experiences annoy you and why?

• What situations have happened where everyone said _____ would happen, but your experience was _____.

• Why was your experience better or worse than what people said it would be?

• What type of information would have helped you to make the experience different?

• Does that information currently exist anywhere?

• What do people always come to you for? (For example, advice? Help on a resume? Restaurant recommendations?)

• What are the little moments at work or in life that give you a rush of happy energy?

Once you start writing these down, you will find new memories popping up or things that annoy you daily. From that, a lot of interesting ideas will come up that may not be businesses, per se, but have the potential to solve a problem, which is a good place to start.

Again, this exercise isn't about going out and exe⁻cuting an idea right away. It is more of a way to show you that you do, in fact, have ideas and interests that could potentially turn into something more. It's important when you are writing down the ideas to not focus on trying to find the perfect solution. Or any solution, really. Just focus on broader ideas or concepts for now, and use the suggested resources in this chapter to expand on the idea.

Get outside of your comfort zone and explore a range of possibilities

As the ideas start to form, begin doing research on the possibilities. When I began thinking about leaving my corporate job to pursue blogging and other creative ideas, an entrepreneur friend of mine recommended that I check out Marie Forleo's website for inspiring and practical advice. In addition to her weekly mailing list and new podcast, Marie runs short YouTube video segments with a tagline, "The place to be to create a business and life you love."

I also listen to at least one business, en⁻trepreneurial, or TED Talks podcast a day, and it has really opened up my eyes to the different ways you can be creative, earn a living online, and pursue new careers.

I write down any and all ideas that come to me, regardless of how feasible they are. It's a great way to get thoughts out of your head, and it's fun to realize that there are so many things you can do.

Some of my favorite podcasts include:

- Authority Self-Publishing
- Brilliant Business Moms
- Creative Calling
- How I Built This
- Marie Forleo
- Pat Flynn Passive Income
- Side Hustle Nation
- Side Hustle Pro
- The Tim Ferriss Show
- Tony Robbins

Some of these resources may not be immediately relevant to you, but it's amazing how much I continue to learn by listening to these! They open up a whole world of options, and I can easily listen to the podcasts when I am out on a walk with my daughter or watching her play.

One tip on podcasts, it's easy to get overwhelmed, so I always read the episode titles and the descriptions first and then pick 1-2 episodes to listen to. If I don't like the host's style after that test run, I move on to a new podcast.

And yes, I included Tony Robbins. I sort of knew who Tony Robbins was, but I made a lot of negative assumptions about him until I reluctantly watched his documentary, *I am Not Your Guru* on Netflix. His message and approach (in small doses) can be incredibly motivating.

I have also watched a lot of inspiring videos, but these are some of my favorites (just search for the ti⁻ tles on YouTube).

- Steve Jobs' 2005 Stanford Commencement Ad⁻ dress
- Shawn Achor: "Before Happiness" (long but a lot of gems in there)
- Tim Ferriss's Top 10 Rules For Success
- Steve Harvey "Jump"

Assess your strengths and skills.

I stumbled across the *Strengths Finders 2.0* book by Tom Rath when I was still trying to figure out what to do career-wise after I left my job. I found that the book helped me to articulate my strengths in a very practical way. You can find summaries of the different Strengths Finders categories by searching online.

Without even taking the test, you should be able to see if some strengths immediately stand out. From there, ask yourself how this strength could manifest in the ideas you wrote down earlier. For example, if "Communicator" is one of your strengths, how could that apply to executing one of the ideas you wrote down? How would that same idea be solved if your strength were "Connectedness"? I did this same exact exercise and loved it because it gave me new ways of thinking through solving a problem or idea.

There are literally hundreds of books for new entrepreneurs, but I think it's important to start with books that are focused and simple, so that you don't get overwhelmed.

Here are some of my favorites:
- *The Art of The Start* by Guy Kawasaki
- *The $100 Startup* by Chris Guillebeau
- *Crush It!* by Gary Vaynerchuck

Don't quit your day job…yet.

Starting a business or, as many people call it, a "side hustle" while you are pregnant or a new mom can be stressful and unpredictable, so keep the full-time income flowing as long as possible. Even with a full-time job and a partner at home, you can still make time to pursue a side business that gets you learning and thinking about ways to monetize your ideas, even if you only spend a couple of hours a week on the idea.

One of the advantages of having a side business while you work full-time is that you don't have the pressure to financially succeed right away. You may find it takes 2-3 iterations or ideas to really get going, but it is very possible to work full-time and spend 5-10 hours a week on a side business that generates income and gets your feet wet into the whole entrepreneurial world.

This advice also applies to stay-at-home moms who want to bring in additional income. Dream big, but also be realistic about what you can take on day-to-day while you work to attain your goals. I constantly have to remind myself that it took me almost 15 years of working to make my highest salary, so trying to replace that in 1-2 years is unrealistic. Not improbable, but I shouldn't expect that to be the norm.

"Don't. Give. Up. There have been so many times where I completely doubted myself only because the expectations I put on myself were too great. It took me almost a full year to get to the point where Take 12 was ready to launch, and there were many instances in that year that I considered throwing in the towel. If you believe in something and you have tested it and you know it is a sound idea, do not let your own expectations get in the way.

I am also a HUGE podcast fan, as I drive a lot. My favorites are The Tim Ferriss Show, How I Built This (NPR), Start Up, Motivating Mom, EOFire, and The Rachel Pedersen Show

Listening to these podcasts has given me not only some great advice and business tips, but they've also helped me stay motivated and focused. It's like surrounding yourself with all of the experts in your chosen field on a regular basis."

~ *Margi Scott, Founder of Take 12 Maternity Registry*

"I would advise any mom looking to start a busi⁻
ness to talk to their local SBA, SCORE, or SBDC
office about what it takes to really create a stable
business. Be realistic about the financial considera-
tions. If you need a lot of capital to start the busi⁻
ness, make sure you can still pay the rent and buy
food before you throw everything into creating
your dream company."

~ Kristine Golden, Founder of Milla-Beyond Maternity

"I have an online women's accessory store that I
was thinking about starting prior to getting preg⁻
nant. I decided to open the store after I had my
baby because I wanted to generate more income.

My advice is to go for it now because there will
never be a perfect time. Always remember why
you started your business because there will be
some tough roads ahead, and your "why" will
keep you focused on your goal.

Don't forget to do your research - Google was and
still is my best friend and I will also search You⁻
Tube when I want to learn something.

Finally, don't allow other people's opinions to de⁻
ter you from starting. You may have to stay up lat⁻
er or wake up earlier to make it all happen, but it is
definitely possible to succeed.

~ Jennifer Hooks, Founder of Chic Society Boutique

Resource Spotlight: Brilliant Business Moms

The following interview features Beth Anne Schwamberger, Founder of Brilliant Business Moms podcast, where she interviews mom entrepreneurs who are succeeding in online business.

What was the inspiration for Brilliant Business Moms?

Brilliant Business Moms started as a podcast in June of 2014. My sister and I came up with the idea after struggling to grow our planner Etsy shop and mom blog, and wishing we could pick the brains of other successful mompreneurs to learn how they were growing their businesses with little ones at home.

We couldn't find a podcast out there interviewing the kinds of moms we wanted to learn from, so we decided to solve our problem ourselves! Luckily for us, it seemed to solve the problem for a lot of other women out there, too, and our listenership grew pretty quickly.

What was the catalyst that made you go from having the idea for a podcast or planner to actually taking the steps to make it happen?

The fact that in both cases, my sister and I were solving our own problem—that was a huge motivator for us to get going and take action. We were just so excited to put the podcast out into the world. And when it came to developing our successful line of planners for mom entrepreneurs, same thing. We couldn't wait to get it into our hands and use it.

Here's my tip for taking a great, big, impossible task and getting it done: Break it down into tiny steps! For both projects, we had a huge list of tasks we needed to accomplish and things we needed to research and figure out.

We divided up the list, and every day we tackled just a little bit more. You'll be amazed at what you can accomplish over time when you take one small step forward each day.

What advice do you have for news moms who are thinking about starting their own businesses?

Every mother-baby pair is different. What works for some may not work for you.

The "work while your kids are napping in the afternoon" works for some moms, but not others. Maybe you're super exhausted by that point in the day and need a nap yourself. Then perhaps waking up early in the morning and working while nursing your baby is a great solution.

Maybe you plan to work three days a week for three hours a day, and let your clients know your boundaries. Maybe you're a baby-wearing ninja, and you can tuck that kiddo in a wrap, and be a productivity goddess! Get creative, and figure out what works for you.

Another tip: build—and use—your village. If you have friends or family willing to help, accept it. They can come hold your baby while you work!

Finally, move at the speed of your baby. Celebrate all the little milestones and wins. Don't rush progress in the first year. Have very realistic expectations, and plan lots of time for self care. By making sure your family is strong and healthy, you'll have a great launching pad for a successful business.

What Brilliant Mom podcast episodes would you recommend for new or expectant moms?

- Busy Blogger Finds Balance
- Connecting Others
- I Love Planners
- Nurturing a Business and a Baby

Do you have any favorite books, podcasts, or motivational personalities that you reference when you need to tackle a business problem or need an extra boost of motivation?

I love the *Online Marketing Made Easy Podcast* by Amy Porterfield because she's always featuring fabulous, step-by-step case studies and actionable advice. Amy makes tackling any new business project feel easy. I also love *The Art of Paid Traffic* by Rick Mulready because I'm constantly inspired to try new things when it comes to online advertising.

In terms of personal support, help, and motivation, I'm really blessed to meet monthly with Crystal Paine of MoneySavingMom.com and brainstorm with her plus get great advice. She's an experienced, brilliant business owner with a big heart, so I know the advice I get from her is solid and trustworthy.

And that's my advice for every mom trying to grow a business: Find an accountability partner or business buddy you can mastermind with. This business thing is hard! You need all the support and encouragement you can get.

Mom Spotlight: Hallie, New Mom + Entrepreneur

Hallie Fenton, Co-Founder of Baby's Choice

Baby's Choice offers a Bottle Bundle box that in‐cludes 4 unique baby bottles and nipples of vary‐ing shapes and sizes.

The idea came about in the middle of my maternity leave. I was breastfeeding my daughter one night and texting my sister-in-law about how she wouldn't take a bottle and just how frustrating that was. I really needed a break, but because she wouldn't drink from the bottles I bought her, my husband was never able to feed her a full meal.

My sister-in-law experienced a very similar thing, so we were texting about how crazy it is that no one talks about babies rejecting bottles and how it's even crazier that a simple variety pack doesn't ex‐ist!

And that's when we decided to create our own.

Working during maternity leave.

I felt a bit of a void while being on maternity leave. I hate to say it, but I kind of missed working. Being a parent is a challenging and rewarding experience but in a very different way than traditional work is.

My daughter was and continues to be a great sleeper, so I'd find that on certain days she would be napping for several hours, and I wouldn't have much to do.

Working on Baby's Choice during those times defi‐nitely filled that void for me, helping me feel more like myself while I was at home.

Making it happen.

At first, my sister-in-law and I just kind of joked about starting our company. But the more we talked about it, the more it became real. I think there were moments when it seemed crazy—why would two women with full-time jobs and new babies want to start a new side business that would require start-up costs?

Ultimately, we felt it was a unique idea that could truly help new moms, so we decided to forge ahead with our plan.

My advice would be that the only way to make it work is if you are really passionate about your idea. For me, my side business is a fun and exciting venture. It's easy to put pressure on yourself to send out a certain number of emails, follow up with a certain number of people, etc. But if you're feeling overwhelmed and unhappy, you've lost sight of why you're doing it in the first place.

New moms have enough to worry about, so don't overload yourself.

Balancing Motherhood with Ambition

I originally wrote the following reflection for my blog, but I wanted to share it in this book because I received a lot of messages from other new mompreneurs that were experiencing similar challenges trying to balance it all.

I constantly struggle to balance my ambitious, business-minded identity with being a stay at home mom. For the most part, my corporate roles allowed me to use my education, training, and professional experiences to solve new problems.

While most of these problems were not that interesting or meaningful, I did enjoy coming up with different types of solutions, which in turn kept my mind sharp. Philly Baby Bump was a nice complement to my job because it gave me a creative outlet, but I only dedicated a few hours a week to it.

Once I became a stay at home, however, the boundaries between working were not so easy to define. For example, while I wasn't working as much during the day, I was working during naptime, the occasional quiet morning, and late at night. And I worked. And I worked some more, because I genuinely loved testing out new ideas and being able to create what I want, when I wanted. But along the way, I lost some perspective and forgot about the stay at home mom part.

I often felt like being a mother was taking time away from my blog, this book, and other business ideas. I was frustrated that my daughter needed my attention (shocking, I know…), even though I had a ton of work to do. I would go to sleep anywhere from 1:00 a.m.-3:00 a.m. and wake up a couple of hours later, tired and cranky or "crusty," as my nephew would say.

It was not sustainable, and as 2016 came to a close, I made the choice to re-evaluate my attitude and reframe the way I was approaching being a mom/entrepreneur. I made a clear choice to prioritize being a mom first.

Practically speaking, this means I now ask myself every morning, "How can I be the best mother today for my daughter?" and then create and adjust my daily to-do list with that context in mind. For me, being the best mother means being present and able to enjoy the little moments with my daughter.

For example, instead of working until 3:00 a.m. several nights a week to complete items on my to-do list, I now limit myself to 2 nights a week where I work past midnight. The rest of the nights, I put my daughter to bed at 6:30 p.m., enjoy dinner with my husband, work for an hour or so, reconnect with my husband to talk or listen to a podcast, and then I go to bed between 9:00-10:00 p.m.

I also stopped regularly waking up at 4:00 a.m. to work. While I could do that in the past when my daughter woke up between 7:00-7:30 a.m., it was no longer possible when her schedule inexplicably changed to 5:30 a.m. wakeups. I was in denial for a couple of weeks but started feeling frustrated and resentful when she would wake up, so I knew I had to stop those early mornings. The extra 45-60 minutes of productivity was not worth being tired and annoyed all day. So until her schedule trends back to waking up after 7:00 a.m., there will be no early mornings.

With this new schedule, I am actually enjoying the quiet early morning time with my daughter, instead of feeling as if it's cutting into my work time. I have also scaled down (but not eliminated) projects that are important to me. It's not worth the stress of trying to take on more than I can handle.

The final thing that has helped me to achieve a better balance is "journaling." At first, I was skeptical because writing in a journal is *not* my thing, but it has been transformational in how I think and approach my day. I use the *5 Minute Journal* that Tim Ferriss made popular, and the journal is a wonderful reminder of all the things I have to be grateful for on a daily basis. I even added a personal section called the "Best of Both Worlds," where I write something great that I experienced as mom that day *and* something great that happened as an entrepreneur. It sounds silly, but it is a powerful exercise when you do it daily.

All of these changes have forced me to take a step back from my never-ending to-do lists and appreciate the rare opportunity I have to raise my daughter while also working on ideas that I love. I am still a work in progress, but I am very happy with how far I have come.

Part IV: Stories on Postpartum Life

CHAPTER

12. More Stories and Unexpected Lessons

"I regret putting pressure on myself and not rest‾ing enough. I also regret trying to "make things easy" on my husband (for example, trying not to wake him at night, etc.) just because he was going to work, and I wasn't. Maternity leave IS work!"

~ *Marie, age 29, Kentucky*

As I mentioned before, this book doesn't really focus on traditional postpartum aspects of maternity leave. However, I did want to showcase a range of postpartum experiences through mom spotlight stories and note the importance of self-care after your baby arrives.

Mom Spotlight: Elizabeth, Elementary School Teacher

Elizabeth, Elementary School Teacher

On the last day of work before maternity leave, I felt apprehensive about all the unknown that was to come but also very excited to let go of work for a little while in order to focus on and enjoy my life as a new mom! That said, I am a teacher and just as with most of my colleagues I take my career very seriously. I had some real guilt over leaving my students behind for a few months!

Maternity leave expectations:

I did not have many expectations for maternity leave because I wasn't surrounded by many moms who were recently on leave. I wasn't sure what it would be like, but I thought I'd never be bored again. Although that was partially true, I did actually feel very lonely a lot of the time, especially during the day while my husband was at work.

I didn't expect to feel lonely when I was con⁻ stantly needed by and attached to my newborn. I wish I'd had some kind of a strong parent network to bounce things off of, pose questions to, and just hang around with.

My husband and I felt very clueless and isolated during my daughter's first year!

Unexpected lessons:

On the positive side, I did not expect to be able to let go of work so comfortably! I thought I would be obsessed over what I was missing at work and what was happening with my students as far as regression or progression. But I was able to let go of work for a little while and really focus more on my new family.

My biggest regret is not enjoying the last few weeks of leave, as I was so incredibly anxious about returning to work and leaving my baby behind!

Mom Spotlight: Alison, Writer

Alison, Writer

On my last day of work, I was exhausted, stressed, and overwhelmed. I had begun working from home a week earlier, but instead of projects winding down (as promised) my work kept ramping up.

Unexpected lessons:

I started my maternity leave a week before my due date but the baby was late,, and I actually had to be induced a week past my due date. I then spent 5 days with my daughter in the NICU. I was stressed and unhappy about "wasting" 3 of my precious 12 weeks.

I didn't expect maternity leave to go by so quickly. I was very anxious about learning the ropes and having time with my daughter before going back to work, finding childcare, etc. It would have been nice to have a few more weeks before going back to work. Our nanny is wonderful, but I still struggle with not being there for my daughter every day.

Best memory:

Having my family around me as my daughter slept on my chest.

Mom Spotlight: Lucy, Communications + Marketing

Lucy, Sr. Communications & Marketing in Non-Profit Education

I was nervous, anxious, very sad, and feeling guilty on my last day of maternity leave. Sad because I was letting my baby down by going back to work. Sad that my child was just starting to be "fun" and becoming more active right when I had to leave her with someone else every day. And guilty that someone else would be "raising" my daughter for me (or so I felt).

I want to be home with her as much as possible and am always running out the door at work to pick her up from the sitter.

Unexpected lessons and regrets:

I regret that I didn't force my husband to be more "hands on" with her. I am paying for that now, by being the full-time caregiver while working 40 hours a week, as well.

However, learned I am more maternal than I thought I was and a hell of a lot stronger than I thought I could be. My mom died a week before I went back to work, so it was a hectic time.

Mom Spotlight: Kristin, Nurse Practitioner

Kristin, Nurse Practitioner at a Large Hospital

I'm now a mom of two, but for my first baby, I had no idea how hard it would be. Experienced moms already know that, but new moms don't. I wish I'd known how hard it was going to be ahead of time.

I thought maternity leave was going to be spending time at home with my new baby, going for walks, meeting friends for lunch. In reality, I was tired, confused, constantly crying, and felt isolated.

I hardly left the house for the first six weeks.

Unexpected lessons:

I wish I'd had a group of women I connected with. I went to a few support groups, but the women at the groups seemed to already be friends, and I felt like an outsider. I wish I had tried harder to find mom friends who were going through the same thing I was.

Best memory:

Afternoon naps with my little one. Constant snuggles.

Mom Spotlight: Flora, Registered Nurse

Flora, Registered Nurse at Community Hospital

I prepared myself that breastfeeding might not work out and told myself ahead of time that I would not let it get to me if it didn't. Well it turns out that just breastfeeding my daughter wasn't working and she was losing too much weight.

I didn't expect to feel so guilty—as if it were my fault she was dealing with all this. We had to sup‐ plement every other bottle with formula, and each scoop of formula made me feel as if I was giving her poison. I know I wasn't, and I never expected to feel that way—but I did. Baby girl is just fine now, and she still nurses at times, drinks both for‐ mula and expressed milk.

Unexpected lessons:

I wish I had consulted a lactation specialist way earlier in my journey. It turned out that my daugh‐ ter has a posterior submucosal tongue tie, so she couldn't get all of my milk and would get tired. If I would have talked with the consultant initially, I would have gotten busy pumping much sooner and saved us both the frustration.

CHAPTER

13. Self-care

"Be kind to yourself. Don't blame yourself for things that don't work out the way you planned and don't feel bad for feeling sad, disappointed, or overwhelmed."

~ Stacy, age 32, New York

Mom Spotlight: Nicole, Physician Liaison

Nicole, Physician Liaison for a

Children's Hospital

I wish I would have relaxed a bit more during my maternity leave, asked for help, actually accepted help that was offered to me. Most importantly, I wish I would have let the dishes, laundry, and my email/Facebook alone and just napped when I could. The lack of sleep really turned my world upside down.

Challenges:

I was plagued with profound postpartum anxiety and depression shortly after having my first son. I was living four hours away from family and many longtime friends during that time, and my husband and I were "blessed" with a colicky baby. I resented friends who talked about how "wonderful" the newborn period was or how they could "be a stay-at-home mom forever" with their seemingly perfect children. I spent most of my leave mourning the loss of what I thought my leave would be like as I tended to a very fussy, challenging baby.

I ended up taking 6 months off (mostly unpaid) due to a handful of issues (postpartum depression, baby resisting to drink from a bottle, irritable and colicky baby, etc.) that I couldn't imagine a caretaker having or wanting to deal with everyday.

Biggest regret:

My biggest regret is that I didn't stay at home when I really wanted to while I was on maternity leave. I was living in the city and had a few girlfriends I had become close with from prenatal Pilates. We all had kids within a few weeks of each other and made lots of plans to get together while on maternity leave. It seemed as if every day I felt pressured to do something with someone.

Instead of relaxing at home and snuggling with my newborn son watching movies, I had created so much anxiety about getting showered/fed and nursing/changing the baby to get out the door to meet my friends. It was hard for me to get out of the house, and I really pushed myself.

My baby didn't nurse well outside of the house, and he cried a lot, so that was an extra layer of un⁻necessary stress I was dealing with on a daily basis.

Returning to work:

When I was in the throws of postpartum depres⁻sion and anxiety—without really knowing it yet—I spoke to a co-worker on the phone.

My son was about four months old, and I had just extended my leave another six weeks. He was a very high-needs baby so I was very overprotective of him and I didn't let many people hold him. It was exhausting but I fully took that on. I just felt as if I was the only one to comfort him.

The job I once loved so much meant nothing to me. I wanted to be home. I believed that no one else would be able to handle his fussiness as his own mother could. My co-worker was a mom of two boys, and I was crying through my sleep depriva-tion, telling her I didn't think I could go back to work.

She was very direct with me and said, "You have to come back. You owe it to yourself to at least try it. You love this job and need a bit of your life back." She gave me the spark...the encouragement I needed to give it a try, and I realized I started to feel better after I went back to work. I pushed through the transition and ended up thriving again at work soon after I returned.

A new perspective.

Only when my second son was born did I realize how much I could actually enjoy the newborn pe-riod. Every child has a different personality and different needs. I learned that maternity leave doesn't last forever, and neither does the newborn period. I wish I had enjoyed it more the first time around.

Expert Advice: Self-care Tips from Diana Spalding

The following postpartum advice is from Diana Spalding, a Founder of Gathered Birth, which offers childbirth education and parenting support.

Plan to take care of you.

You're probably spending so much time thinking about and planning for the baby's arrival and making sure everything is perfect for him or her. But don't forget to plan for yourself, too! You've been working so hard growing your baby and will work hard giving birth to your baby; you will need a lot of tender loving care after birth, as well.

Prepare a freezer full of meals, so you don't have to cook—or better yet, ask your friends to do this for you! Pre-schedule times for friends and family to come over to clean, cook, or hold the baby so you can shower and nap. Create a little nook for yourself where you can just relax and nurture yourself after birth. Really focus on healing and honoring yourself for this amazing thing you are doing—becoming a mother!

Be gentle on yourself.

You are allowed—and encouraged—to be amazed by yourself and to treat yourself with love and gen‐ tleness. For the weeks after your birth, your only job is to heal and to care for your baby. Those are pretty big jobs, in and of themselves, so don't worry about jumping back into the swing of things right away. Take your time, and marvel at your awesomeness.

Remember your hormones.

Your body will experience tremendous shifts in hormones following the birth of your child, and these can cause some pretty big feelings. The first few weeks after having a baby, many women experience the "baby blues"—feeling ecstatically happy one moment and then totally overwhelmed and tearful the next. This is normal, to a point.

If you find that this is lasting for more than a few weeks, or the sad/anxious feelings are consuming you, seek help from your doctor or midwife; this could be postpartum depression, and we can help you feel better. And if you worry that you are going to hurt yourself or your baby, call 911, or go to the emergency room.

Assemble a team, and use it.

Adjusting to motherhood is huge; it's amazing, yes, but it can be really hard, too. Spend some time forming a team of people who can help you after the baby comes. Call a lactation consultant to help you get breastfeeding off to a good start (many are cov‐ered by insurance). Don't be afraid to call your pediatrician with questions (I promise your questions are not silly). Consider hiring a postpartum doula to help you transition into this new lifestyle. Remember that there are many professionals around you who want to help you—you are not alone.

Beware cluster feeding.

Perhaps the thing I hear most from new moms is, "Why didn't anyone tell me about cluster feeding?" If you will be nursing, you will experience periods of cluster feeding when your baby eats constantly. It can be very draining and frustrating, but know that it is normal, and it will pass. When your baby goes through growth or development spurts, they will be extra hungry and in need of comfort, so they will nurse often. But usually, this only lasts for a series of days, and then things return to normal.

Nobody really knows what they are doing:

I say this not to scare you but to inspire you. When I had my first baby, I remember looking at everyone else around me, assuming they all had it completely together, knew exactly how to be perfect parents, and never struggled or doubted themselves. Three kids later, I can say with confidence that this is just not the case. Everyone has self-doubts. Everyone has bad days. Everyone has questions. So if you feel as if you are fumbling a bit, it's okay. You love your baby more than anyone on Earth, and therefore, you are already a fantastic mom. Trust yourself, and enjoy your journey. You're going to be amazing.

My First 30 Days Postpartum

I was (or thought I was) overly prepared for the birth of my daughter. I had my hospital bag packed and on standby in the living room weeks before my due date. I even had a "birthing kit" neatly packed that included two different types of heat packs: one that I could plug into a delivery room outlet and another, microwaveable rice-based heat pack that I could use in case to walk around and help with labor contractions.

The only thing that I procrastinated on was the nursery but in the final stretch of pregnancy, the "nesting" bug that I had heard about finally kicked in and we did the nursery in one weekend. The point is, I am a planner. But I was strangely and maybe just wonderfully naïve about what happens after you bring home the baby.

The following are 3 tips on how to survive those first 30 days, based on my experience.

Stock up your freezer and pull out the crockpot or Instapot!

I ended up eating grapes for dinner one night when my husband was out of town for a conference. Clearly, food is one area that I grossly overlooked when I had visions of what life with a newborn involved. We were incredibly fortunate to have friends and family cook and bring us food, so that wasn't the issue.

The issue is that the food didn't last forever. In our case, it lasted about a week and a half, and then all of the groceries I bought prior to giving birth started to dwindle! We tried going to Whole Foods and getting groceries, but then that actually involved cooking what we bought. We tried ordering Blue Apron meals, but again, that actually involved cooking. So then we tried eating out and ordering in dinner, but that quickly became very expensive to do after the third week. Thus, grapes for dinner.

My husband and I both really enjoy cooking, so I guess we never anticipated how much the exhaustion would affect our desire to cook. If I had to do it over again, I would cook a ton of freezer-friendly dinner meals ahead of time and probably buy one of the Instapot cookers that almost every mother I know raves about!

If you don't have enough space in your freezer, ask a friend, family member, or neighbor you are close to if you can use some of their space. They won't mind and will be happy to help, because let's be honest, offering space in their freezer is infinitely easier than your friend actually having to cook for you. You can then spend your money on breakfast and lunch by either buying groceries that don't require actual cooking, such as yogurt, fruit, salad, sandwiches, etc. or treating yourself to a casual meal out.

Find your version of a croissant and coffee date

After the adrenaline of birth and having a new baby started to wane a little, I was sort of taken aback at the repetitive nature of the first 30 days. Since I was breastfeeding every 2 hours, there wasn't much energy or time to do anything else.

Whether it was 4:00 p.m. or 4:00 a.m., you could usually find me in my robe or yoga pants, doing one of three things: nursing, changing, or taking a catnap with the baby. The only real exception was that every morning for at least the first 2-3 weeks, my husband and I walked two blocks to our favorite coffee house —Greenstreet, for those of you who live in Philly— and ordered iced coffee and chocolate croissants and sat outside in the sun (it was summer). While simple, these dates allowed me to get some fresh air, to indulge in two things I gave up during my pregnancy, and frankly, to break up the monotony of a newborn's daily routine.

I highly encourage new parents to do something that involves leaving the house daily for the first 30 days. Even if it's just a walk around the block after dinner or listening to music while you sit on a park bench. The type of activity doesn't really matter, and it doesn't even have to be exercise-oriented. It just has to allow you to breathe for a moment and internally process this new life.

Let others help you.

No, really. Politeness doesn't win points here, and trying to be a perfect mom this early is the quickest way to drive you to insanity. Consider the first 30 days after birth as a grace period, and save the dream of perfection for later! What this means is that when friends and family come over and ask how they can help, do not turn them down! They want to help, and you need all the help you can get. Not sure how to respond? Not a problem. Here is a list of suggestions:

- "Can you watch the sleeping baby so that I can take a glorious, twenty-minute shower?"
- "Can you hold the baby, so I can enjoy—and even finish—my cup of coffee while it's still hot?"
- "Can you take the dishes out of the dishwasher, and put the dirty dishes in?"
- "Can you fold the clean clothes that are in dryer?"
- "Can you vacuum the living room for me and lightly sweep the kitchen floor?"
- "Can you put the baby bottles in soapy-hot water for me, so it's easier to rinse them later?"

Final Words of Advice

I conducted a survey last year of new moms in Philly and this was the one response that *still* res⁻onates with me. I hope you take it to heart because it is the best advice I have heard so far about maternity leave.

"When you get home, let the house fall apart, ignore your phone, and just snuggle with that little one. The world can wait"

Thank you for reading
The Insider's Guide to Maternity Leave.

If you enjoyed this book and found it helpful, I
would greatly appreciate a review on Amazon.com.

FREE!

Sign up and receive a free digital file that includes the
resources, checklists, and links featured in this book.

www.TheInsidersGuidetoMaternityLeave.com

VICTORIA HEFTY

I am the author of *The Insider's Guide to Maternity* and the founder of Philly Baby Bump, an award-winning blog for new and expectant parents, and an MBA graduate from The University of Chicago Booth School of Business. Most importantly, I am wife to an incredibly supportive husband and mother of a charming and precocious two year old.

If you have any questions or constructive feedback, please email me at **victoria@phillybabybump.com.**

Made in the USA
Monee, IL
14 December 2020

52799915R00105